# RUGBY
## REMEMBERED

# RUGBY REMEMBERED

FROM THE PAGES OF

DAVID PARRY-JONES

PARTRIDGE PRESS

LONDON   NEW YORK   TORONTO   SYDNEY   AUCKLAND

TRANSWORLD PUBLISHERS LTD
61–63 Uxbridge Road, London W5 5SA

TRANSWORLD PUBLISHERS (AUSTRALIA) PTY LTD
15–23 Helles Avenue, Moorebank, NSW 2170

TRANSWORLD PUBLISHERS (NZ) LTD
Cnr Moselle and Waipareira Aves,
Henderson, Auckland


Published 1988 by Partridge Press
a division of Transworld Publishers Ltd
Copyright © Text: David Parry-Jones 1988
Illustrations: Illustrated London News

Designed by Graeme Murdoch


*British Library Cataloguing in Publication Data*

Parry-Jones, David
Rugby remembered: from the pages of the
Illustrated London news.
1. Rugby football, history
I. Title    II. Illustrated London news
796.33′3

ISBN 1-85225-045-3

Photoset in Linotron Century Old Style by
Rowland Phototypesetting Ltd
Bury St Edmunds, Suffolk
Printed in West Germany
by Mohndruck Graphische
Betriebe GmbH, Gütersloh

# CONTENTS

# Preface

In 1987 pictorial coverage of Rugby football reached a crescendo as New Zealand and Australia jointly mounted the game's first-ever World Cup competition. The action was often breathtaking, the sheer commitment of participants from sixteen nations was never in question, and in the end nobody doubted that the best team, New Zealand, had won.

Furthermore, thanks to zoom lenses, satellites suspended like stars far out in space, and human dexterity applied to television's complex hardware, audiences which could be measured in billions were enabled to enjoy the passionate quest for a trophy appropriately named after William Webb Ellis – who in effect established the handling code with his misdemeanour of 1823.

It is intriguing to reflect how the same ingredients and the same factors have characterised Rugby football's image as portrayed in *The Illustrated London News* for over a century. The determination, the dash, the verve and vivacity of today's Shelfords, Sellas, Kirks and Kirwans are constantly paralleled, from the very earliest "edited highlights" to be found in the magazine's pages right down through the years.

If the game itself manifests consistency, however, the nature of its coverage in the *ILN* is an ever-changing phenomenon with four distinct phases. First, just as snooker caught the imagination of the media and hence the public in the 1980s, so a century earlier Rugby football rather more gradually seized the interest of *ILN* editors as an action-packed pastime ideal for reportage in an organ of pictorial journalism.

Once its appeal was established there followed a period devoted to novelty and experiment, for instance with the selection of touchline viewpoints suitable for artists and photographers and by varying methods of displaying pictures on the magazine's ample pages. In this second era another priority was devising methods of beating competition from daily newspapers. Thirdly, after the Hitler War came consolidation when *The Illustrated London News* (and *The Sphere*, whose library it now owns and from which some of the pictures in this volume are taken) were pace-setters and product-leaders in the quality photo-news field.

But since the late 1960s two factors have forced a major re-think about the magazine's coverage of Rugby football and, indeed, of all big sport. First, the arrival of vivid colour television coverage of the great occasions at Twickenham, Murrayfield, Cardiff and elsewhere presented a new and formidable challenge. Then came the change to monthly publication, placing a premium on space and ruling out the old luxury of full-page photo montages of important matches. The *ILN* pulled in its horns and replaced such full blooded coverage with one-off pictures-for-the-record which had to earn space for inclusion by saluting a Grand Slam or commemorating a royal presence in the grandstand.

I am thus grateful on two counts to the proprietors of the *Illustrated London News* for permission readily given to delve into the magazine's copious and bulging archives: these afford a unique insight into the development of one of the world's great games from crude and humble origins into a globe-spanning spectacle; and they depict an important period in the media's response to the challenge of a pastime that has grown inexorably in appeal and popularity. The rise and rise of the Rugby game perceived in the pages of the *ILN* is undeniably unique.

The ready co-operation is acknowledged, too, of top photographers John Harris, Colin Elsey and the Sport and General Agency, among others, from whose dark rooms have come a number of the studies in this volume's final pages.

David Parry-Jones
Cardiff, 1988

# THE ILLUSTRATED LONDON NEWS

No. 1.]     FOR THE WEEK ENDING SATURDAY, MAY 14, 1842.     [Sixpence

## OUR ADDRESS.

In presenting the first number of the ILLUSTRATED LONDON NEWS to the British Public, we would fain make a graceful entrée into the wide and grand arena, which will henceforth contain so many actors for our benefit and so many spectators of our career. In plain language, we do not produce this illustrated newspaper without some vanity, much ambition, and a fond belief that we shall be pardoned the presumption of the first quality by exalting the aspirations of the last.

## DESTRUCTION OF THE CITY OF HAMBURGH BY FIRE.

By the arrival of the General Steam Navigation Company's boat Caledonia, off the Tower, on Tuesday evening, news has been brought of an immense conflagration which took place on Thursday morning, the 5th instant, at one o'clock, in that city. The district in which the fire broke out consists entirely of wood tenements, chiefly of fire and sea stories high, and covering an area of ground of about thirty to forty acres.

*View of the Conflagration of Hamburgh, from the River.*

# 1
# The beginning

 The world's first newspaper with pictures, *The Illustrated London News*, appeared in 1842. There was a young Queen Victoria to portray, charismatic politicians such as Peel and Disraeli to feature. The spectacle of public hanging was under attack from writers like Thackeray and Dickens. Strikes and lock-outs affected the Midlands and the industrial North Country. In the opening edition of May 14 there were graphic features on a train crash in France, war reports from Afghanistan, one or two book reviews and some fashion notes.

Despite competition from 400 newspapers elsewhere in Britain the new journal sold 26,000 copies, a figure which rose to 60,000 by the end of the year. A rich seam had been struck, and it was clear that the great, grey broadsheets of the day could be challenged successfully by a publication containing pictures.

Preferably, action pictures.

Just nineteen years earlier a sixth former called William Webb Ellis had transformed attitudes to the sport of football by picking up the ball and running with it, presumably earning himself a hundred lines in the process. It would take *The Illustrated London News* another half century to perceive that the 1823 revolution at Rugby School was admirably suited to coverage in its columns.

But then, it took that amount of time to introduce a semblance of order into what became known as "Rugby football".

The earliest pictorial representation of a Rugby football game is a sketch dating from 1839 showing the headmaster of the day, Dr Arnold, and guests watching boys of Rugby School at play. The drawing shown here, however, full of the meticulous detail at which *The Illustrated London News* artists were so adept, is almost certainly the first portrayal of "foot-ball" reproduced in a newspaper or magazine: publication date was February 28, 1846.

It depicts the townspeople of Kingston-upon-Thames staging their annual Shrove Tuesday match in the market place, a right claimed to have been secured through the valour of their ancestors. Tradition relates that a Danish raiding force was defeated at Kingston, after which the severed head of its leader was kicked around the streets. The contestants pictured in 1846 were from two local groups, the Thames-Street Club and the Townsend.

The ball can be discerned close to the head of a man on the right (directly beneath the church tower), and though it has clearly been kicked we may justify the drawing's inclusion if we note that an arm – if not a hand – is being used to control it.

An off-the-ball incident can be spied at far right, where a private feud is clearly being settled, while the top-hatted man in the left foreground evidently requires medical attention.

The accompanying report notes that "the poorer classes play for money and beer". It adds that the annual game "is supported by some of the wealthiest inhabitants in and around Kingston". So they had sponsors then, too.

 While townspeople wrestled and hacked their way across streets and squares in the quest to let off steam, boys at many of England's great public schools were more fortunate. Surrounding them were acres of meadowland which, thanks to imaginative estate management and generous bequests, could be converted into "playing fields" to meet the newly-fashionable craving for exercise as part of the best establishments' curricula.

"The Close" at Rugby School in Warwickshire began as a small plot of land just south of the school buildings. It expanded as the school grew, a space being reserved in its north east corner for the playing of cricket and football. This was known as "Bigside" – and it was here in 1823 that the sixteen-year-old pupil called William Webb Ellis picked up and ran with the ball.

This was strictly against the rules and led contemporaries to comment with faint distaste that Webb Ellis "was generally inclined to take unfair advantages at football". However, his action founded a new sport, or a new "code", and is commemorated on the tablet now fixed to the indented wall to be seen on the right of the above picture.

The scene has an idyllic quality suggesting that, using the practising footballers (an early "squad session"?) to provide human interest, the artist was in this case chiefly concerned to record the school's impressive architecture – indeed a comparison with the second picture suggests that to this end he has actually left out a large tree!

By 1870, however, when the latter picture was published, the intention is clearly to illustrate a highly competitive occasion. Although the participants all wear hoops there are two sides in opposition. The touchline onlookers are

both numerous and captivated by the action, though one young lady is alarmed by the collision that has taken place beneath her gaze. The portrayal of the adjacent boy confirms that at Rugby School handling had by now won acceptance: he has been "collared", or tackled, and has lost possession.

It is interesting to speculate on the ball's nature. The Gilbert firm, whose founder William supplied shoes, boots and other leather goods to the school in the nineteenth century, say that by 1870 rubber was taking the place of the age-old (and somewhat unsavoury) pig's bladder in order to inflate the balls made by them (which were blown up by a pump invented locally). They add that the fat oval shape evident in this picture generally did duty at that time, the more pointed ends being introduced some decades later.

Many spectators in the middle distance have encroached onto the area near the goal-post. This is by now H-shaped, indicating the necessity to kick the ball over the cross-bar in order to register a score.

A final observation concerns the way the artist has drawn the score or so of pursuing figures: they have an unrelenting quality that can best be described as "dogged": do we have here the origin of the term "pack"?

THE REV. W. W. ELLIS, M.A. (ST. CLEMENT DANES). FROM
A DAGUERRÉOTYPE BY BEARD.

Ellis is a name that prompts the Welsh to claim the founder of Rugby football as their own; and the Irish say that the great man was born at Tipperary. Unluckily for the Celtic fringe, however, according to information supplied by him to the census of 1851 his birth took place at Manchester, England, in 1807.

A year later Webb Ellis senior died in the Peninsular War. Granted a pension of £10 a year for their offspring William, his widow moved to Rugby to have him educated on a local scholarship. An Exhibition took him on to Brasenose College, Oxford, where he represented the University at cricket. Joining the Church he spent a considerable period of his career in London and appears also to have worked in South Africa. For some years before his death in 1872 he served as a rector in Essex.

Unsuccessful efforts were made to discover his last resting place in time for the Commemoration Match of 1923 in which an England–Wales Invitation XV beat Scotland–Ireland 21–16 on The Close. It was a further thirty-six years before the indomitable researcher Ross McWhirter found his tomb at Menton, south east France, where he evidently died while on holiday. The French Rugby Federation has since refurbished the grave and adorned it with a marble headstone.

From time to time during the later years of the nineteenth century the founder was criticised by his contemporaries who all but called him a cheat. Perhaps, after he "took the ball in his arms and ran with it" he had to endure a few days' ostracism. But, ultimately, there may well have been a deputation of fellow footballers who approached him with the olive branch, "Webb Ellis, about this exciting new Law you want us to introduce . . . .".

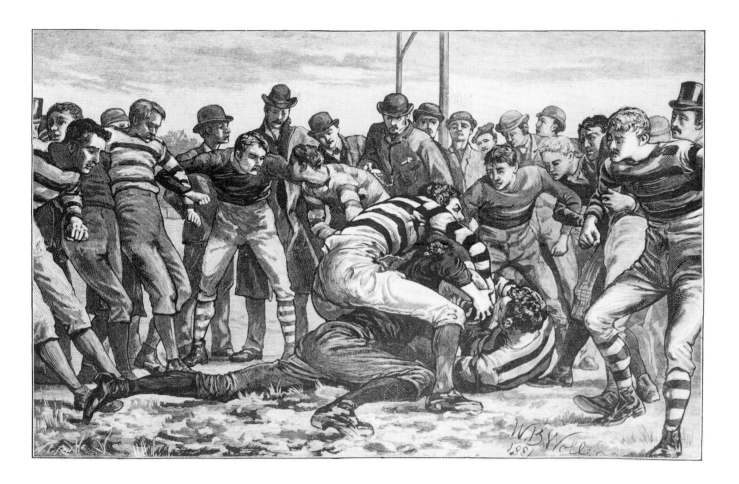

 It was the natural instinct of Rugby School's old boys to preach and if possible demonstrate the merits of football as they had learned to play it; that is, with its distinctive handling dispensation. Thus from limited beginnings the game began acquiring a larger following, which *The Illustrated London News* felt impelled to assist. It accompanied this drawing with the comment, "Mothers, sisters, aunts and female cousins of enthusiastic players will require a few words of explanation."

So do we, a century later. Fortunately the magazine explains the roles of the participants: ". . . three of them grappling together on the trampled turf while others, with linked arms, form a circle around the holder of the ball to prevent him from breaking out and running away with it if he should elude the grasp of his wrestling foes."

However, the need was felt for a homily aimed at the anti-Rugby faction who highlighted the game's "mimic strife" and the serious injuries that can be incurred by players. Says the *ILN* columnist, "These accidents do not kill or permanently disable for life; and though a kick on the shins is extremely painful the risk of it should deter no valiant youth from taking his due part in a manly social exercise admirably suited to call forth those sterling moral qualities: self-devotion, quick resolve and prompt decision, courageous instant action, persistency, endurance and the habit of combination with others for a common purpose."

So there.

The astonishingly rapid spread of the Rugby game is nowhere better attested than in this illustration published in 1875. It shows a game in Calcutta, whose Football Club was founded in December 1872. Not surprisingly an Old Rugbeian, G.H.R. Hart, was among the first members, who soon totalled 130. There were two seasons: June 20 to August 31, the "rains"; and November 14 to February 28, the "cold", when temperatures stayed down at 70°F.

"Football," the caption-writer assured his readers, "is now one of the most popular games in Calcutta, matches having been witnessed by the Governor General." Here, the British Raj is epitomised by the couple at the left (backs to the sun); while the native presence may be discerned on the far touchline.

But sadly the boom could not last, and by 1877 James Rothney, captain of the "CFC", was writing to inform the recently-founded Rugby Football Union in London that the Calcutta club had gone out of existence. He blamed competition from polo and the dispersal or posting home of many old members who had started the club.

Calcutta's connection with the game, however, has endured. The same letter offered the RFU a sum of £60 – the CFC's assets at dissolution – to pay for a challenge trophy to be competed for in any way deemed best for the encouragement of Rugby football.

The money paid for the "Calcutta Cup" – for which England and Scotland have competed hotly for over a century.

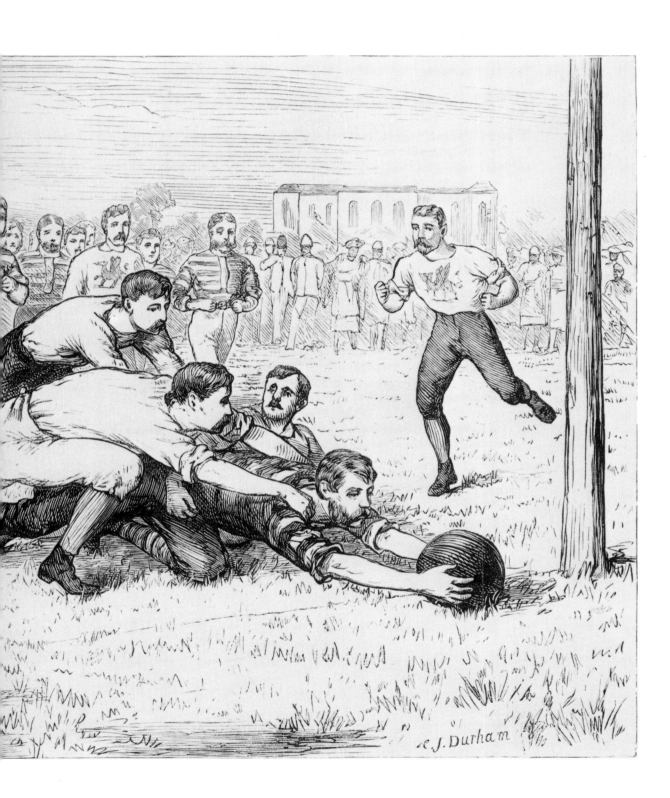

C.J. Durham

It is 1887, and the Press has realised that the new sport which began at the schools, was organised by Rugby, caught on at locations as diverse as Blackheath, Edinburgh, Llandovery and Calcutta, and was eventually formalised with the foundation of the Rugby Football Union in 1871, far from being a hole-in-the-corner pastime for muddled oafs, is actually capable of attracting crowds of spectators – and thus worthy of extended coverage. On his assignment to a fixture in a pleasant, suburban setting, the artist A. Forestier pictures onlookers at least two deep along sectors of the touchline.

These are important sketches for several reasons. All participants are shown wearing breeches, yet by the end of the decade shorts had largely taken their place.

Bearing in mind that in the early days clubs each brought an umpire to fixtures, it is interesting to speculate on the roles of the two characters in plain clothes. Soon, when umpires disagreed as vehemently as players, the appointment of independent officials became necessary: here one such authority-figure appears to be overseeing the scrummage with a languorous air (though he clearly has no hope of keeping up with any back play which may develop).

"Umpires" continued to attend matches but were now relegated to policing the fringes rather in the manner of the gent with the walking stick. They survive as today's touch-judges.

Finally, note what may be the first depiction of a line out. This method of returning the ball into play from touch had received general approval in the 1860s.

# THE ILLUSTRATED LONDON NEWS

REGISTERED AT THE GENERAL POST-OFFICE FOR TRANSMISSION ABROAD.

No. 2582.—VOL. XCIII.　　SATURDAY, OCTOBER 13, 1888.　　WITH EXTRA SUPPLEMENT } SIXPENCE. By Post, 6½d.

The Two Umpires

The "Surrey Team" cheering the "Maories" on their appearance

Their War Cry before starting Play.

The first Goal for New Zealand.

A sudden outburst of Joy on getting the 1st Goal of the Tour.

Mobbed. 3 Cheers for the Visitors. Hip Hip &c &c.

The visit of the Maoris in 1888 was not only the first inward tour by a national group to the British Isles; it remains one of the most astonishing the game has known.

Supplemented by four *pakehas*, or white men, the Maoris came to reciprocate a British team's visit to New Zealand made earlier the same year. They played 107 matches (a modern tour side might play 22 at a pinch) winning 78, drawing six and losing 23. Most of their games took place in the north of England, where crowds may well have been bigger, but in October they played Surrey in front of a sizeable gathering whom they saluted with a war-cry before the kick-off: an early *haka*, but evidently watered down somewhat for European scrutiny.

"All black" is the team colour selected for this pioneer New Zealand tour side. Maybe it was cheap, could be ordered in bulk and washed easily; but for whatever reason it certainly caught on as all the world was reminded in 1987.

Surrey's players doff their caps to their guests. Another sartorial note concerns the shorts which, compared with *The Illustrated London News*'s picture coverage of twelve months earlier, have now replaced breeches.

 International football took off nearly as far as you can get in the British Isles from Rugby School. Raeburn Place, Edinburgh, was the venue for the match between Scotland and England in 1871, and the majority of Scotland's matches between then and the end of the century returned there. England's policy, however, was peripatetic, games against the other Home Countries being staged at Richmond, the Oval, Manchester, Dewsbury, and Blackheath, where *The Illustrated London News* gave the visit of Wales full-page coverage in 1892.

Quite obviously the game had "arrived" as a major spectacle, and the crowd shown at the Rectory Field is not only large but wildly enthusiastic as the visitors' line is crossed – the scorer must be Alderson, Evershed, Hubbard or Nichol. Clearly the conversion will be a formality, contributing to a 17–0 victory.

It is tempting to assume that the Welsh tackler is the redoubtable Jack Bancroft, while somewhere in the foreground may lie Arthur Gould, described as late as 1948 by the critic Townsend Collins as "the greatest Rugby footballer who ever played". Well, that may be true but this was still a year when the Welsh lost all their three matches.

Though there is no sign of him, the referee was a Scot, Mr M.C. McEwan. It may be that the artist forgot to include him – for the *ILN*'s pictorial accuracy was not infallible: in the team photograph, shown opposite, the England side wear white shorts!

 By 1892 there was nothing new about photography in the Press. The *ILN* had been using it since the middle of the nineteenth century and had pioneered a process which blended it with wood-engraving. It remained, however, a ponderous craft for many years, so that artists with sketch-pads continued to hold sway along the touchlines of a fast-moving, unpredictable sport like Rugby football. On the other hand, the camera was undeniably better for taking team portraits.

Caps are still being worn, with a few exceptions. Players sport roses on the breasts of their white jerseys, though their design could hardly be called uniform, and indignant Irish readers might be forgiven for spying plants that look more like shamrocks, especially in the case

of F. Evershed (standing, right).

Dress apart, the players have a curiously modern look about their expressions, on which shows that pent-up blend of latent aggression and tension common to all teams in all decades just before the kick-off of a big match. The lens is now the cynosure of attention, and only A. Allport (right, seated) looks away.

This XV, all northerners from Lancashire and Yorkshire, with the exception of four Blackheath representatives, was exceedingly successful. After their victory over Wales they proceeded to win a Triple Crown, defeating Ireland 7–0 and Scotland 5–0.

Following the formation of the Welsh Rugby Union in 1880 (the game had been popularised in the Principality by graduates returning from Oxbridge) matches with England began in 1881, the senior nation winning seven out of the first nine encounters with one draw. A 12–11 reverse at Cardiff in 1893 stung the English to emphatic retribution in 1894 when they won by twenty-four points to three.

It may well be that *The Illustrated London News*, along with other organs reporting Rugby football, were now being required to annotate their illustrations of play much more comprehensively. The caption accompanying England's first try is notable for the reporter's expert recall, never an easy skill to cultivate before the arrival of action replay on television.

"A magnificent piece of play," he writes. "Wells at last came away with a fine run, three parts the length of the field, and when collared, passed to Hooper; who transferred, when a few yards from [the] goal line, to Murfitt, for the latter to run in between the posts." A splendid début, then, for the man from West Hartlepool, excellently presented by the *ILN*'s page-designer (though England's full back, at right, does not exactly look like a forerunner of R.W.H. Scott or J.P.R. Williams!).

By 1894 Rugby football had taken on board two important reforms. One concerned the tackle law, which was amended in 1887 to say that, once held, a player had to release possession, which immediately led to a more fluent, open game.

The other concerned the three quarter line, which Wales had experimented with as early as 1886 through the influence of Frank Hancock, an early captain of Cardiff RFC. The change involved fielding eight forwards and seven backs (as opposed to a nine–six division), and by 1893 most clubs and countries had accepted it.

Thus we can be fairly sure that the ball-carrier in this instance, C.M. Wells (Harlequins), was the England stand off half. The caption in *The Illustrated Sporting and Dramatic News* (whose library, like that of *The Sphere*, is owned today by the *ILN*) is not specific, but it is tempting to draw the conclusion that the break by Wells is the one described in the previous picture as leading to Murfitt's try.

Contemporary reports say that Birkenhead was invaded by the Welsh, who may have come across the Dee from Clwyd and Gwynedd to cheer their compatriots from Cardiff, Newport, Swansea, Llanelli and other outlandish places. This was the one and only occasion for an England–Wales game to be staged at Birkenhead, though oddly enough Wales had played Ireland there in 1887 "to minimise the travelling costs of the IRU who, at the time, were feeling the pinch" according to the International Championship's historian Terry Godwin. (Why not Fishguard? Or Milford Haven?) On that occasion Wales won fairly comfortably.

Wells

the Welsh Backs.

Reporters frequently berate sub-editors and caption writers for the liberties taken with their copy and pictures (usually, it has to be said, by reason of the pressure under which they have to work). However, one wonders what, in this case, Mr W.B. Wollen thought of the line "Well saved: Hard lines" that appeared beneath his illustration of 1893.

He had clearly gone to great lengths to show a splendid try by the team in plain jerseys, with a sweetly-timed scoring pass delivered by the man on the ground. There is no way the hooped defender can prevent the ball-carrier going in under the bar. The caption writer cannot have been familiar with Rugby football.

Although the games of Association and Rugby football were fast gaining in popularity, they were still relatively obscure and outlandish activities to the average metropolitan journalist. It is even conceivable, therefore, that the office staff-man thought he was writing about soccer (the better-known of the two codes) and that the goal-keeper had just brought off a fine save!

Also intriguing is the statuesque pose of the referee compared with the speed and momentum of the game itself.

In March 1901 a crowd of 18,000 came to Blackheath for what *The Illustrated London News* saw as a "tie-breaker". That is, in the preceding years each nation had won nine of the twenty-seven matches, with the remarkably high proportion of nine draws (five of which contained no score at all).

The crowd saw a quite magnificent display by Scotland, who achieved their highest winning margin over England with an 18–3 victory which included four tries, one of which is surely about to be scored by Gillespie, Welsh, Timms or Fell with the Scot on the right about to put in a little constructive obstruction.

The action has clearly appealed to artist Allan Stewart (with a name like that, maybe the result did too). Thus it is curious to reflect that it took the *ILN* thirty years to make up its mind to look in on a Calcutta Cup match and acknowledge the commitment and popularity of fixtures between England and Scotland.

The surroundings at Blackheath show marked evolution compared with earlier studies. Not only has a terrace of houses sprung up in the distance, but also a covered grandstand has been provided for wealthier paying customers – such as Lord Rosebery who, the *ILN* noted, attended Rugby matches at this time.

By 1902 Wales had embarked upon what is fondly recalled as their first "Golden Era", but England fought to the bitter end before conceding defeat by 9–8 at Blackheath. The Welsh success presaged a Triple Crown campaign.

Here the *ILN* and its artist Ralph Cleaver demonstrate unerring journalistic sense by featuring centre-page "The penalty kick which gave the victory to Wales." John "Strand" Jones of Llanelli is the kicker – evidently the Paul Thorburn of his day, able to kick vital points under pressure. And clearly matches were decided by penalties in the good old days too!

Cleaver's powers of observation were impressive, as shown in a series of cameos which surrounded his main drawing. Particularly good is the study of the Welsh scrum half – not named, but actually Dicky Owen of Swansea – whose technique is a model of excellence (and reminiscent of the recent All Black Dave Loveridge). Owen's balance is good, so that he is unlikely to be bowled over prematurely by an opponent and the ball is obviously about to speed on its way propelled by a flick of powerful wrists needing no delaying wind-up.

The study "Taking a place-kick" is also notable for the concentration on the participants' faces and for the delicate sketching of the kicker's right hand which has just completed its final adjustment.

Observe, too, the "Welsh method of expressing delight". Coaches returning down the M4 after a Twickenham victory are still packed with fans who doff bobble-hats to the pavements or conduct impromptu choirs!

TAKING A PLACE KICK

A TRY FOR ENGLAND

DESTRUCTION OF OUGHTRED'S SHORTS

GAMLIN GAMBOLING

THE PENALTY KICK WHICH GAVE THE VICTORY TO WALES

A QUICK PASS FROM SCRUM.

KIPLING'S "MUDDIED OAFS"

WELSH METHOD OF EXPRESSING DELIGHT

The handling code had been imported smoothly and fruitfully into Oxford and Cambridge with the inflow of Old Rugbeians, and the *ILN* traditionally saluted games between the two universities. The Varsity match of 1902, which inspired Ralph Cleaver's illustration of Oxford's second try, ended in a draw with each side scoring a goal and a try.

This series started in 1871, just after the first international match between England and Scotland. Since 1920, of course, the venue has been Twickenham; but before that matches took place at Oxford and Cambridge, the Oval, Blackheath and, from 1887 to 1919, Queen's Club.

Players' dress is broadly the same as that worn today, with the exception of the stockings: those worn by Cambridge today feature the pale blue and white hoops of the jerseys, while Oxford's no longer feature hoops at all.

Maybe the cheering fans portrayed by Cleaver are Old Blues from an earlier era.

Producers of televised Rugby matches invariably feature the Kew Gardens "pagoda" in the middle distance to indicate that the cameras are at Old Deer Park or Richmond. In 1903 Ralph Cleaver used the self-same landmark to cover a game in which Scotland beat England by ten points to six to regain the Calcutta Cup.

It is interesting to reflect that one of the eager Scots about to seize the luckless English ball-carrier may be John Dewar Dallas who refereed the Wales–New Zealand match at Cardiff two years later and has been vilified for most of this century by irate Kiwis for disallow-ing an equalising "try" by Bob Deans which would have preserved the First All Blacks' unbeaten record.

Certainly Dallas scored in this match, when he won his only cap; and far from being the old fogey figure painted by New Zealanders as unable to keep up with the play, he was only twenty-seven when he ruled against Deans and almost certainly well-placed.

Who is the Englishman? Given the circumstances and the cut of the hair it could well be full back H.T. Gamlin of Devonport Services, the senior player on the day.

 At regular intervals in its history Rugby football has experienced upheavals amounting to revolutions. In 1987 New Zealand won the game's first-ever World Cup competition by what, in retrospect, was a wide margin of skill and commitment. The same country's First All Blacks of 1905 were equally far ahead of their time. They played a different ball game.

When their Test against England loomed up on December 2, 1905, the unbeaten record boasted by the visitors drew a crowd of 50,000 to Crystal Palace (according to *The Sphere*, whose handsome wide-angle view of the scene is now in *The Illustrated London News*'s possession), where England were defeated by fifteen points to nil. This was not a giant total compared with those recorded elsewhere on tour, but nonetheless it comprised five sparkling tries scored in what were described as "swamp-like"

conditions – perhaps not surprisingly, since the Rugby pitch was laid out on the filled-in site of a former artificial lake.

Sidney Paget's drawing, accorded the rare status of a double-page spread, includes the first recorded instance of a police officer on match duty, doubtless enjoying his afternoon out while keeping an eye on the crowd – some of whom have shown enterprise by bringing stools to stand on. Packed grandstands, often framed by ornamental canopies, occupy the middle distance beneath the Crystal Palace's misty silhouette.

In one respect the picture is startlingly modern, and depressingly so to Europeans. New Zealand's forwards are "hitting the ruck" (to employ today's terminology) with bodies low and plenty of combined power. Their opponents, in contrast, are upright, spread out and generally disorganised.

 Not to be outdone *The Illustrated London News* went for a two-page drawing by Ernest Frater, who clearly sat opposite his rival from *The Sphere*. This drawing was probably inspired by the early stages of the game when "England's attacks were spirited"; but the expression worn by the New Zealander about to catch the ball is one of calm confidence, and there seems little doubt that the ball is about to be booted safely away to touch.

This picture is notable for an innovation in the form of the identifying captions which appeared above it in the magazine. Fred Roberts, for example, is on the receiving end of a desperate pass from Jim Hunter. At far right is Bob Deans,

fated to score the disallowed "try" against Wales a fortnight later. Most significant is the grim figure wearing a bandit moustache in the middle of the drawing. This is New Zealand's tour captain Dave Gallaher, described as a "winger". This does not mean that he played on the wing; rather it was an early term used to describe a loose forward who could leave the pack to handle and tackle with the backs. The British were not too sure about the ethics of this kind of play, and Gallaher was constantly at the centre of controversy.

But, down the centuries, innovators are usually the winners. And they call the shots.

 With the unique victory over the All Blacks safely in the record books, Wales had confirmed themselves as the leading Home Country of the early twentieth century. For season after season Triple Crowns and Championship titles fell to Gwyn Nicholls and his men.

The Springboks' 1906 victory at Swansea therefore ranks as one of the great upsets of Rugby history. They won convincingly by a goal and two tries (eleven points) to nil, the first success by visitors on Welsh soil since 1899. The Rugby world was stunned; South Africa had arrived as a Rugby nation; and the seeds had been sown of an inferiority complex towards the Springboks which the Welsh have never thrown off.

Paul Roos is remembered as a founding-father of South Africa's Test Rugby: scatter-brained and unpredictable as a youngster; sage and sensible in middle age as an MP; opportunist and quick to learn in between as captain of his country.

We reproduce the line-out picture because, for the first time in the *ILN*, jerseys are shown bearing numbers. This innovation may derive from the necessity for players on a long tour to wear their own garments to ensure a good fit; or else it may have been through increased public curiosity about players' identities. The other action pictures, however, simply indicate inexperienced cameramen's problems in deciding where to position themselves to obtain the maximum return from their negatives.

The goal-kicker photographed at practice is Dougie Morkel. His timeless posture is strongly reminiscent of "Okey" Geffin's style nearly half a century later (except that the latter's place kicks usually got airborne!).

Hard on the heels of the tremendously successful New Zealand side of 1905 came the First Springboks, Die Spring-bokke. Although Rugby football had been played in South Africa for a quarter of a century, skipper Paul Roos stated modestly when his side arrived at Southampton in autumn 1906 that his side had "come to learn".

Not long into the tour, on November 17, that modesty did not seem misplaced. Scotland provided the South Africans' first Test opposition and won comfortably before 40,000 ecstatic Glaswegians by two tries to nil. Apart from the vainly jumping Scot in the foreground, the line-out at which the Springbok thrower-in is aiming appears likely to be a vastly more orderly affair than would be the case later in the century.

"The visitors never seemed like winning for a moment," observed the *ILN* reporter. Nevertheless a week later South Africa were in Belfast defeating Ireland by fifteen points to eleven. And the best was yet to come.

SOUTH AFRICAN TEAM

SEASON 1906-7

ENGLISH TEAM

SEASON 1906-7

THE ENGLISH TEAM AT THE CRYSTAL PALACE

F.J. DOBBIN

H.A. de VILLIERS

J.W.E. RAAFF

W.A. MILLAR

H.C. DANEEL

S. MORKEL

S. JOUBERT

A.F. MARSBURG

D.J. BRINK

P.A. LE ROUX

D. MORKEL

J.A. LOUBSER

D.C. JACKSON

S.C. de MELKER

SPRINGBOKS NEARLY OVER THE LINE: JACKSON CLAIMS A TRY.

AFTER THE HEEL OUT: SCRUM BREAKING UP

LINING OUT FOR A THROW IN.

JACKETT HURT TRYING TO PREVENT SPRINGBOKS FIRST TRY.

CARTWRIGHT KICKS OFF

HEELED OUT: A DASH FOR THE BALL.

P. ROOS

A THROW IN: MARK YOUR MEN

The South Africans completed an arduous programme of four Tests on successive Saturdays by holding England to a 3–3 draw. Their tour, with its record of twenty-five wins from twenty-eight games, steadily captured the public's imagination which is reflected in *The Illustrated London News*'s coverage of three Tests.

The photography is credited to three sources, but the picture montage again shows the difficulty encountered getting into the right place at the right time. Thus the South African try has just been missed. The photographer has arrived in time to snap England's forwards bending sympathetically over Edward Jackett who was hurt in an attempted tackle on the scorer. However, the line out picture and the shot of players hot in pursuit of a loose ball are well taken and well selected.

The nickname given by Paul Roos to his players, Die Springbokke, was seized upon by graphic artists to decorate page margins.

The Kew pagoda makes its obligatory appearance in this fine study by F. Leist which graced the cover of *The Graphic* (another defunct magazine whose archives now rest safely in the *ILN*'s vaults). The date is October, 1908, and a third great southern hemisphere nation, Australia, is on its first tour of the Mother Country. In the match pictured here a London XV were beaten by one try to nil.

The position of the touch-judge, lurking near the posts, suggests that there has been an unsuccessful penalty kick at goal which is being cleared by the tourists' full back Philip Carmichael. He and his team-mates sport the Waratah, a common flower in New South Wales, whose 1927 Rugby tourists in Britain wore it as an emblem. It seems that the Australians had not agreed upon a tour nick-name before leaving home; and only in response to demands from the British Press for them to emulate the "Springboks" was the unofficial title "Wallabies" adopted.

Both Carmichael and his opposite number got a good write-up on this occasion. The latter, Lieutenant G.O. de H. Lyon, RN, had actually set sail from Chatham but "by the kindness of the naval authorities a torpedo boat was sent for him and he was overtaken near Spithead and brought up to town by a special train."

 Lt. Lyon went on to play in England's Blackheath defeat by the Australians; and if he was playing in the game pictured here he was on the losing side yet again. An Army player is held by Royal Navy defenders during the two Services' encounter at Queen's Club in 1911 when victory went to the landlubbers by twenty-two points to thirteen.

This time the artist is Ernest Frater, whose portrayal of the hand-off and the victim's anguish is particularly effective.

More than a touch of class distinction is detectable in the caption, deriving, of course, from the occasion itself: "There is no finer match to be witnessed in London than that between the officers of the two Services." Aye aye, sir.

Wales have never beaten South Africa, and despite high hopes in the Principality the 1912 Test was to prove another victory for the Springboks, this time by just a penalty goal to nil.

The centre-piece illustrates a "pile-up" as impressive as any witnessed during the 1970s; and the tourists were clearly prepared to enter the maul in true kamikaze fashion to judge from the horizontal shins at right. Possession is going South Africa's way thanks to the tight forward's strength and determination to rip clear.

In the background the artist has included the first pavilion to be built at Cardiff Arms Park (on right with pointed roof). Not to be confused with a grandstand, it contained changing rooms for players using the Rugby pitch and adjoining cricket field, and was equipped with shower-baths and a gymnasium.

Wales had their chances, and a drop at goal by H.W. Thomas (Swansea) would have won the game had it been successful since such scores were then worth four points. But Boetie McHardy had a near miss at the Welsh corner flag, too, the ball slipping from his grasp.

F.J. Dobbin was a most distinguished early Springbok. Besides touring the Home Countries twice he appeared against British Isles' sides in South Africa in 1903 and 1910.

G. MORKEL STEADYING HIMSELF IN THE MUD.

H. W. THOMAS'S DROP AT GOAL WAS PERHAPS THE MOST DESERVING OF SUCCESS OF ALL THE GOOD THINGS THAT NEARLY CAME OFF.

DOBBIN.

M°HARDY LOSES THE BALL WHEN WITHIN A FEW FEET OF THE CORNER FLAG.

MIGHTY TACKLING WAS THE OUTSTANDING FEATURE OF THE GAME.

MILLAR

F.C. PUTTER-IRWIN (THE REFEREE)

VILE (TOWARDS THE END OF THE MATCH)

KNIGHT.

A PROBLEM FOR THE ENGLISH SELECTORS. WHO SHALL OPPOSE STEGMANN?

GOOL PLAY BY WILLIAMS

MARK! (BIRT)

 What a contrast with the pre-match build-up to modern Test Rugby and its huddles of tense players, arms wrapped around team-mates, studiously ignoring the opposition. Here England's selected XV of 1913 rub shoulders with their South African opponents before the kick-off – surely a rapport bound to contribute to an excellent on-field atmosphere.

The captains, N.A. Wodehouse and Douglas Morkel, are seated at centre. Second from left, also seated, is the legendary Harlequin R.W. Poulton (later Poulton-Palmer), rated by many of his fellow countrymen as the best back produced by England up to this time. Alas, the brilliant centre met his death in World War I.

 This match, which the Springboks won 9–3 to complete a Grand Slam over the Home Countries, marked the first appearance of Twickenham in *The Illustrated London News*. The photographer initially takes up his position at the south east corner of the ground, which had been purpose-built by the RFU as England's headquarters and opened in 1910. South Africa were the first visiting nation to beat England at the new stadium.

There had evidently been concern at crowd behaviour on recent occasions, and the *ILN*'s caption writer is moved to congratulate the onlookers at Twickenham: "They cheered both sides with equal heartiness, received the decisions of the referee with respect and showed by their behaviour that they did not begrudge the Springboks their victory."

Later, the cameraman, enigmatically named as "C.N.", moves to the touchline and snaps the break-up of a scrummage with England's scrum half bending to retrieve a not particularly good ball. "C.N." has adopted a crouching position which heightens the scene's intrinsic drama. This is enhanced by the page designer's choice of a linear frame for the action.

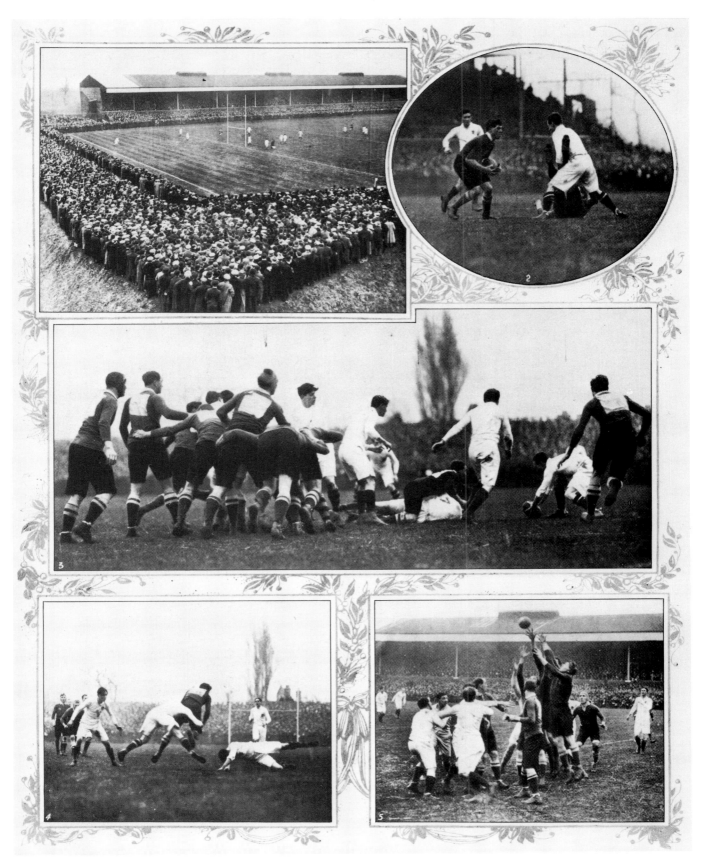

It is 1914 and photography has been around for a long, long time. But still men sent with cameras to Rugby matches cannot guarantee their editors significant shots of the moments that really matter in any sporting contest – the scores.

The reason is partly because they lack the experience possessed by today's experts which, allied to a sixth sense, prompts them to be in the right place at the right time. But secondly, whereas the significant action in Association football and cricket takes place in sharply focused areas – around goal-mouths and at the wicket – Rugby football has goal-lines measuring some seventy-five yards, or seventy metres, where tries can be scored.

So right up to World War I artists are still entrusted with the portrayal of tries; and this is D. MacPherson's impression of "Cherry" Pillman's try under the bar which Fred Chapman converted to snatch victory over Wales in 1914 by ten points to nine. Just as today's reporters are not too proud to watch TV recordings to ensure accuracy, so one imagines that MacPherson took the trouble to check their positions with the players involved to supplement his own recall of the circumstances.

The aghast figure at right is Jack Bancroft who allowed a kick to bounce over his head for Pillman to win a race against frantic defenders, the nearest of whom is (left) Willie Watts.

The Press called this "a match for the gods". Certainly some of Rugby's eternal verities are captured in the drawing.

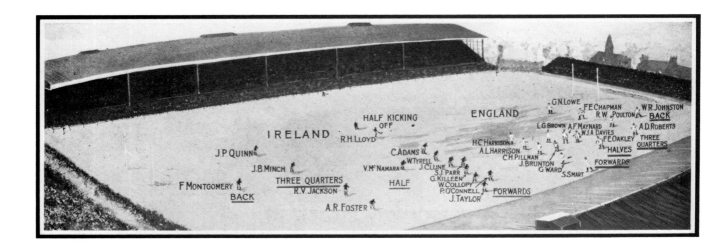

IRELAND

ENGLAND

HALF KICKING OFF

R.H.LLOYD

J.P.QUINN

C.ADAMS

W.TYRELL

J.B.MINCH

V.Mc NAMARA

THREE QUARTERS

J.CLUNE

S.J.PARR

R.V.JACKSON

HALF

G.KILLEEN

W.COLLOPY

P.O'CONNELL

J.TAYLOR

F MONTGOMERY

BACK

A.R.FOSTER

G.N.LOWE

F.E.CHAPMAN

R.W. POULTON

W.R.JOHNSTON

BACK

L.G.BROWN

A.F.MAYNARD

A.D.ROBERTS

W.J.A.DAVIES

F.E.OAKLEY

THREE QUARTERS

H.C.HARRISON

A.L.HARRISON

C.H.PILLMAN

J.BRUNTON

G.WARD

S.SMART

HALVES

FORWARDS

FORWARDS

C.N.LOWE    A.L.HARRISON    S.SMART    H.C.HARRISON

IRISH GOAL

DAVIES OBTAINS BALL FROM A SCRAMBLE

POULTON

CHAPMAN

LLOYD

A DODGING RUN FEINTING TO PASS BUT RETAINING POSSESSION

ROBERTS

MONTGOMERY

SCORES BRILLIANTLY BEHIND THE POSTS

DAVIES

 England were to beat Scotland narrowly and France comfortably in Edinburgh and Paris to round off the 1914 Championship season, but their 17–12 victory over Ireland in February was secured in the last international match to be played at Twickenham before World War I. King George V (at a Rugby match for the first time since his accession) and Prime Minister Asquith were among the big crowd who saw England's second win of what turned out to be a Grand Slam campaign. In *The Sphere* the match was accorded right royal treatment with innovative use of graphics (top).

The side-on view is representational, and though the artist may have checked names and positions with the two captains his prime purpose is to indicate the broad deployment of participants at the kick-off for the benefit of those unfamiliar with the game.

Another diagrammatic impression shows how W.J.A. Davies, the England stand off half, ran brilliantly through the Irish defence to score a try at the posts which Chapman easily converted. Again this seems to be an instance of a magazine editor determined to portray for his readers a climactic moment from the game.

According to R.C. Reed, whose match report accompanied the illustrations, Davies sold two dummies on his way to the line, with Poulton acting as a useful decoy runner.

What with such spectacle and the fierce forward exchanges captured by the touchline photographer the King must have enjoyed his afternoon in the grandstand.

 It is worth noting at the end of Section 1 how *The Illustrated London News* had from time to time taken a sidelong glance at the game in America. The motive was mainly curiosity; but an element of concern is unmistakably present lest the development of Rugby Union football in Europe and the Empire should be affected by the baser, more brutal character of the game that was evolving in the United States. (It is fair to add that the Americans themselves were alarmed about it ever since the young Franklin Roosevelt was badly hurt in a game.)

This picture (above), "from an instantaneous photograph by J. Burton, New York", was published in 1897. Instead of "well stopped, sir", "hard luck!" or another bland cliché the caption writer chose the words "Three-to-one: collaring a half back", thereby managing to inject a faint note of distaste at the perceived absence of a sporting approach.

Note the face-protector worn at left, the thin end of an armour-plated wedge.

By 1910 heavily-armoured Rugby players had become the norm on the other side of the Atlantic, and Cyril Cuneo's cover picture for *The Illustrated London News* of November 26 is clearly designed to convey an alien, even nightmarish, image.

Two United States warships, the *Idaho* and the *Vermont*, were in London that autumn, and their crews had agreed to stage a demonstration of American Rules Football at Crystal Palace to allow the British public to judge the sport for itself.

It failed to catch on as a sport at the time (and has not done so to this day despite Channel Four TV's success in exploiting it as entertainment). Probably the reason had to do with the British working class's already firm allegiance to Association football, coupled with the distaste of public school "hearties" for the wearing of protective clothing – "not on, old chap". Shin pads and scrum caps (later headbands) have been the sole "armour" condoned by Rugby footballers.

However, the *ILN* was quick to salute what it considered to be legitimate American innovation, such as the tackle-bag practice drawn by Russell Flint in 1905 (above).

# 2
## Between the wars

Some charity and inter-Service games were played during the 1914–18 War, but only half-heartedly: the scything down of Britons in their prime on the battlefields of Europe seemed to render the "mimic strife" of Rugby football faintly obscene. As a Scot wrote, "No field game was more thoroughly represented in France, Gallipoli and Mesopotamia, to say nothing of the High Seas, than Rugby football, but the toll exacted for patriotism was a heavy one. Scotland lost no less than thirty-one International players."

England lost R.W. Poulton-Palmer, killed in Belgium, as well as J.H.D. Watson, who had come into International football with a great flourish as the former's midfield partner during the 1914 season. Among the Welshmen who died was C.M. Pritchard, mortally wounded in a raid on the German trenches in 1916: "Have they got the Hun?" he asked as they bore him to a treatment post. "Yes," someone told him. "Then I have done my bit," were his last words.

The Irish, too, were hard hit. When the International Championship began again in 1920 they found themselves pressed to field a National XV worthy of the name – they lost all four matches in that first campaign.

However, public enthusiasm for spectator sport, as would be the case again in 1946, was enormous after the enforced stoppage, and *The Illustrated London News* was not slow to acknowledge it. Although caricaturists occasionally visited Rugby football's great stadia, pen and ink had now surrendered pride of place to the camera; and it has to be said that by 1920 the camerawork is more assured. A few years were to go by before the problem of photographing tries would be cracked, but close-ups of tough touchline exchanges were now captured confidently on celluloid, and this assurance was matched by the positive picture selection and lay-out of the page-planners.

And to add spice to the Championship in Europe a new force was emerging upon the Rugby scene.

Curiously *The Illustrated London News* ignored the re-start of International Rugby in January, 1920, including England's match at Swansea where they lost to the eventual Championship winners Wales. However, the difficulty experienced by Scotland in Paris, when they scraped home by just a goal to nil, ensured that cameramen were present on the touchline at Twickenham where the Tricolours were the first post-War visitors.

In the opening decade of the century the French had learned to expect hammerings by thirty or forty points, and even after their admission to what became the "Five Nations' Championship" in 1910 no immediate improvement took place in their performances. Thus a substantial crowd turned up to see if the narrow defeat by Scotland had been a mere fluke; suffice to note that the home team won a tense game 8–3 against a nation that the *ILN* pronounced "must be reckoned with seriously in International football". France scored try for try, the place-kicking of England skipper John Greenwood securing victory for his team.

Greenwood appears in the frieze of portraits with which the *ILN* chose to decorate its match coverage. Wavell Wakefield, soon to grip English Rugby by the scruff of the neck and transform its potency, is also featured. Another interesting character is Frank Mellish, whose Rugby history was indeed chequered: educated in Cape Town, he came to England for a spell in his twenties and won six caps from Blackheath before returning to his native country where he played half a dozen Tests against New Zealand and the British Isles. He is further remembered in Europe for managing the outstanding tour by the 1951 Springboks.

In the pre-War years France's shadow tackling had been notorious, but the action captured by photographer "C.N." shows a new-found determination to put men on the deck and also to contest possession at mauls.

The 15,000 spectators "cheered the Frenchmen loudly at the close" we are told by the caption writer.

DURING THE GREAT MATCH, WHICH ENDED IN A WIN FOR ENGLAND: FRANCE TACKLING

KEEN PLAY DURING THE GAME: A TUSSLE FOR POSSESSION OF THE BALL.

 Compared with his grand-daughter and numerous other members of today's Royal Family King George V was less of a race-goer than a football fan. A few days before paying this visit to the Varsity match he had been at Stamford Bridge watching Chelsea in action, and we have noted that he had watched England at Twickenham immediately before the outbreak of war in 1914.

Here he shakes hands with the Oxford captain, D.D. Duncan, who was to lead the Dark Blues to an exciting 17–14 victory over Cambridge in the last match of the series to be played at Queen's Club before the move to Twickenham. A duckboard has thoughtfully been provided for His Majesty whose shoes retain their shine; and he scorns the spats affected by the spectator in the foreground.

The King's presence inspired the players to tremendous heights of endeavour, and the score-line contained no fewer than eight tries.

A page full of photographs of considerable significance appeared after England had beaten Wales to start a Jubilee season ultimately distinguished by a Grand Slam. But Wales had won at Swansea the previous season and there was doubtless relief as well as jubilation in the heading "The Downfall of the Leeks".

As it turned out, in 1921 England were embarking upon one of their best-ever decades, one in which they were to win the Championship five times with only sporadic interruptions from the Celtic fringe. The doughty Wakefield was joined by Tom Voyce in a formidable pack which was constantly nursed by what critics described as "the best pair of half backs England ever had": Lt. C.A. Kershaw and Lt.-Com. W.J.A. Davies.

"Before the match," the caption writer informs us, "a Welsh enthusiast climbed one of the goalposts and placed a bunch of leeks on top, but in sliding down he brought the leeks with him – an evil omen." To be sure! – England won by eighteen points to three.

From the magazine's point of view it is interesting to note that "C.N." has now been joined by "G.P.U." and this revolutionary two-camera coverage paid off. One of the pair decided to post himself close to a corner flag where, first of all, he was able to record A.M. Smallwood's near-miss and then – wonder of wonders – to produce the *ILN*'s first authentic photograph of a try-scorer *in flagrante delicto*: C.A. Kershaw is fairly rocketing clear of the visitors' defence to collect a sparkling first try for England. Wales look suitably dumbfounded.

When scrum half Pierre Berbizier was directed to throw in from touch by France's coach of the 1980s Jacques Fouroux, this was greeted by the Rugby world as a revolutionary move, a tactical innovation (though of debatable value). But the third photograph by "C.N." or "G.P.U." shows scrum half Kershaw doing just that at Twickenham sixty years earlier.

THE BEST PAIR OF HALF-BACKS ENGLAND EVER HAD: LIEUT. C. A. KERSHAW ("SCRUM HALF") PASSING TO LIEUT.-COM. W. J. A. DAVIES.

THE ENGLISH "SCRUM HALF" (LIEUT. C. A. KERSHAW) THROWING-IN FROM TOUCH AT A LINE-OUT: AN INCIDENT OF THE MATCH.

THE RIVAL CAPTAINS : (L. TO R.) LIEUT.-COM. W. J. A. DAVIES (ENGLAND) AND MR. J. WETTER (WALES).

WHAT IT MEANS "TO GRAPPLE WITH THE FIERCE OLD FRIENDS": THE ROUGH-AND-TUMBLE OF A RUGBY MAUL (UNORGANISED SCRUMMAGE).

SCORING THE FIRST TRY FOR ENGLAND : LIEUT. C. A. KERSHAW (WITH THE BALL, IN LEFT FOREGROUND) OVER THE WELSH LINE.

MR. A. M. SMALLWOOD (WITH THE BALL) NEARLY SCORES FOR ENGLAND : COLLARED ON THE TOUCH-LINE CLOSE TO THE CORNER FLAG.

There is still luck in capturing the split second in which a great try is touched down; but by 1922 it can safely be said that good judgement is being brought to bear as well. The photographer has decided that, despite Scotland's half-time lead, England have something going for them on the right wing where Cyril Lowe is much too experienced for his opposite number. The hunch has paid off and he is beautifully placed to record England's first score. Lowe has placed the ball a moment before being pushed into the corner by a Scots defender. Later Lowe scored again, and a third try by W. J. A. Davies helped the home side to an 11–5 win.

The caption to the second photograph says, generously, "A Scottish player downwards on the ball in the middle of a loose scrum." Forwards from other nations would be more likely to comment acidly, "An early example of the Scots demonstrating their consummate skill at killing the ruck"!

But then, festooned by shorts as long as those on the right, it must have been difficult struggling to one's feet.

Scotland bade a melancholy farewell to quaint old Inverleith as an International venue (Murrayfield was by now an ongoing project) by losing for a third consecutive year to England. The Sassenachs were in rampant form and were destined to complete a Grand Slam by beating France in Paris.

However, at Inverleith England had to give their all to take the spoils by just eight points to six. Archie Gracie, whom Welsh spectators (yes) had carried shoulder-high from Cardiff Arms Park after his winning try there two months earlier, and Edward McLaren got scores for the Scots with Alistair Smallwood replying for England. But it was left to Glouces-

ter's Tom Voyce to clinch victory for the visitors by crashing over for a magnificent try near the posts. The moment is well captured above.

Voyce, say contemporary reports, "knew it all and could do it all. His spoiling work was deadly; his constructive efforts often meant scores for his club, county or country . . . never from any cause – accident, illness, family troubles or business cares – did he miss one of the twenty-seven English Internationals from 1920 to 1926." His versatility is worthy of note, for on the injury-plagued British Isles tour of South Africa in 1924 Voyce turned out on the wing and as a full back.

It took daring on the part of *The Illustrated London News*'s page planner to settle for a right hand sheet with nothing much in the foreground but printer's ink, six minuscule Rugby players and a referee. Surely the effect justifies his boldness, however: the first photographic double-page spread of a Rugby International and a noble portrayal of the sudden way in which the handling game breaks its tight shackles and heads for spectacle and glory.

Scotland are the 1924 visitors at Twickenham where their scrum half William Bryce (also a hockey International) has just been pressurised by Alan Robson. It looks as if he has done well to get a pass away at all; but, sadly, Herbert Waddell on the receiving end looks about to collect both the ball and a heap of trouble in the shape of Arthur Blakiston and Geoffrey Conway. Referee T.H. Vile is well placed to see that no late tackle is perpetrated.

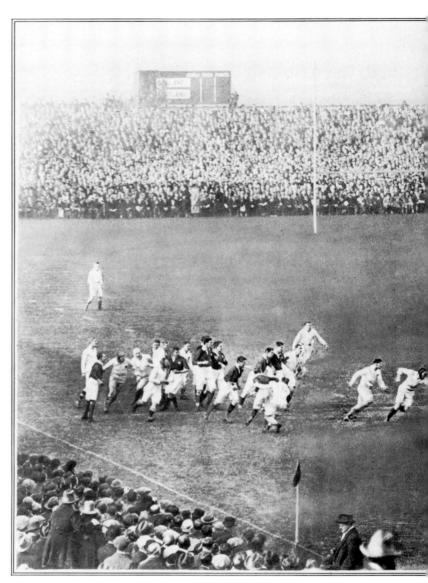

England were continuing their successful decade, the victory rounding off yet another triumphant Championship campaign yielding a Grand Slam. For the Scots, defeated by three goals and a dropped goal to nil, this was a seventh reverse in a row at the hands of the old enemy. The "Oxford Scots" – Smith, Macpherson, Aitken and Wallace – were together in the three quarter line for the first time, but it was to be twelve months before their full impact on European Rugby would be felt.

The home team were led by W.W. Wakefield, whose pack included no fewer than five back row forwards. Perhaps that explains why he himself, a flanker, is third from left in England's line out with Tom Voyce close at hand.

The huge throng on the south terrace were part of a crowd put by the *ILN* at 45,000, a record (yet again the King was there). This encouraged the RFU to build a new north stand in time for the next home Calcutta Cup match.

Excitement reached fever pitch with the visit of the Second All Blacks in 1924. Today's readers, used to annual tours and players who hop the hemispheres as casually as catching a bus, have to remember that no touring side had visited Britain since the South Africans of 1912. How would the Home Countries acquit themselves as the southern hemisphere threw down the latest gauntlet?

Not very well, as it turned out. The tourists played thirty games in Britain and France and won them all; and their virility is vividly and excitingly captured in this superb study of the nineteen-year-old Maori from Hawkes Bay, George Nepia. His was a surprise selection, especially as he had never previously appeared in his tour position, full back. However, his contribution was outstanding. Denzil Batchelor's description of him is memorable: "He was between short and tall, and his thighs were like young tree trunks. His head was fit for the prow of a viking Longship, with its passionless, sculpted bronzed features and plume of blue-black hair. Behind the game he slunk from side to side like a black panther on the prowl."

Pictures can tell stories and, as this photograph underlines, they can sometimes encapsulate character too.

The true Rugby enthusiast has usually been prepared to endure any misery to watch the best sides in action, as is shown by this delightfully tongue-in-cheek photograph from Grange Road (where Cambridge University put up a gallant fight before losing to New Zealand by just a goal to nil). It gains inclusion on merit and also prompts the choice of two more shots showing the game's ever increasing popularity.

The second shows the south terrace at Twickenham crammed to capacity (hats are *de rigueur*). At the top can be seen the simple

score-board which did duty at the time and also the clock tower, taken down in 1950 and replaced by the Hermes weather vane.

However, coincidentally crowd control was becoming something of a headache for the authorities, one that could become acute if a Championship title was at stake. When Ireland visited Cardiff in 1936 both they and their hosts were in with a chance of topping the table, and the number of fans wanting to see the game approached 100,000. By the time apprehensive stewards locked the gates two and a half hours before the kick-off, the *ILN* estimated that

70,000 had got in; and thousands more had to be dispersed by the hoses of Cardiff's fire brigade when they tried to batter down the gates from frustration and disappointment.

The photograph shows the overflow of spectators onto the grass, which caused frequent interruptions to the game while referee Cyril Gadney ordered them back. Less lucky were supporters on the terraces where overspilling caused panic and many were swept off their feet and trampled.

Wales won 3–0, and the all-ticket match had come a day nearer.

 It was the same old story in 1924. Just as they would in 1963, 1967, 1978 and so on critics ascribed a superb All Black tour record to their constant "togetherness" on the pitch, to superior fitness, and to a more considered approach to matches. But in an analytic article of December 1924 "The All Blacks and their Methods" Leonard Tosswill added, "The representatives of the Dominion are a magnificent body of men, full of energy and rejoicing in their strength. They typify the virility and freshness of outlook of their coun-

try . . . The words of their war-cry are not inappropriate seeing what they have accomplished:

☐ 'The New Zealand storm is about to break;
☐ We shall stand as children of the sun;
☐ We shall fly to the heavens in exultation;
☐ We shall attain the zenith!
☐ The power, the power, the power!'"

Even Welsh hymns could not fuel fervour to match this, and Cliff Porter's team avenged the 3–0 reverse of 1905 with an overwhelming victory by nineteen points to nil at Swansea.

Rowe Harding (top left), one of the most polished of all Wales's wings, prepares to cross kick off a crumb of possession; but for the most part the big New Zealand forwards held the whip hand and played their opponents into the ground (bottom, opposite).

Tosswill's article, which speculated on the kind of challenge England would offer the tourists on January 3, 1925, focuses on the All Black "wing forward" (first encountered in 1905) who, he observes, has the job of putting the ball into the scrummage. "This leaves the half back free to receive the ball as soon as it is heeled; the English half back puts the ball into the scrummage and then has to hurry back to the base of the scrum to receive it and, if his forwards heel too quickly, he may be too late to pass it out before he is collared." The photograph makes his point (top).

One wonders, therefore, why so perceptive a tactician as W.W. Wakefield, who led England, did not decide on a huge effort to outscrummage the New Zealand seven with his English eight.

 Twickenham's capacity had been raised to 56,000 for the visit of the All Blacks through the completion of a new North Stand with its single balcony; and it is clear from this fine photograph that every space in the ground was taken to see whether the tourists could preserve their 100 per cent record in their final match in the United Kingdom. Matching popular enthusiasm *The Illustrated London News* went to town on what it called "the most dramatic and exciting match on record", spreading a panoramic view across two pages (which gives a glimpse of Twickenham's East Stand just before the addition of its upper deck).

Drama there certainly was as England first appeared to gain the upper hand but then succumbed to New Zealand's superior drive and dynamic, going down by seventeen points to eleven.

But there was also tragedy, witnessed by the Prince of Wales, who was introduced to the All Blacks by their manager, S.S. Deans, before the kick-off. Scarcely had the royal visitor made himself comfortable in the front row of the stand than Cyril Brownlie, a back row forward, was making history by being sent from the field by referee A.E. Freethy of Neath. A New Zealand Rugby historian has written, ". . . an excitable Welsh referee lost his grip on an early flare-up among the forwards on both sides. When Edwards, the tough man of the English pack, and Cyril Brownlie clashed a little later, he sent Brownlie off." However, before that drastic action Freethy had issued a stern warning to both sides; and after that a referee has no option but to act.

What then happened, as is so often the case, was that the fourteen remaining All Blacks were motivated to play like supermen to overcome the handicap, and the slur, imposed on them – none more so than Brownlie's aggrieved brother Maurice. His solo try, after a charge which reportedly bowled over one Englishman after another, inspired his team-mates to hold on through England's last desperate attacks.

During the twentieth century Scotland's home games had been played at Inverleith with its crowd capacity of 30,000. Just as popular interest had persuaded the English to enlarge and upgrade their ground, so in Edinburgh it spurred the authorities to action. Their response was to establish a new headquarters at Murrayfield, which was opened with the Calcutta Cup match against England on March 21, 1925.

*The Illustrated London News*'s photograph certainly did the big day justice and is a nostalgic reminder of the majesty of Murrayfield's popular bank which spectators scaled like mountaineers (it was super-structured in 1983 by a new £3 million grandstand). This match was seen by a Championship record crowd of 80,000.

For Scotland the occasion could not have been more satisfactory. Beforehand there must have been great apprehension after seven successive defeats by England. In the event, a 14–11 victory ended that malign run; secured the Scots their first Title since 1907; and was the win which gave them a Grand Slam.

The picture shows A.C. Wallace squeezing over at the corner for Scotland's match-winning try (his fourth in four Championship matches), magnificently converted by A.C. Gillies.

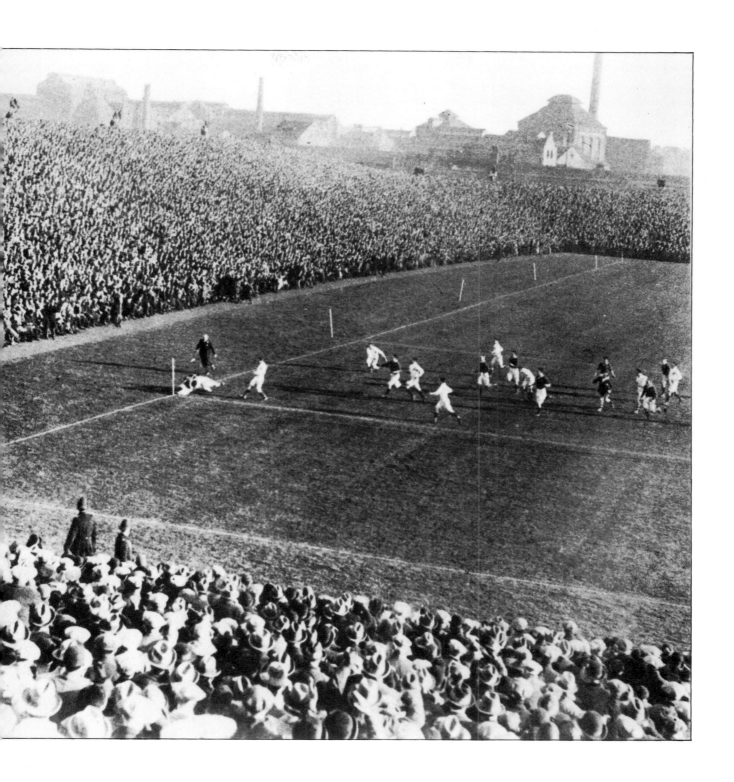

THE GREAT "RUGGER" MATCH WHICH LEFT SCOTLAND STILL HOLDERS OF THE CALCUTTA CUP AND EQUAL WITH IRELAND AT THE HEAD OF THE CHAMPIONSHIP: AN EXCITING MOMENT—WAKEFIELD, CAPTAIN OF THE ENGLISH TEAM (WHITE JERSEYS), BROUGHT DOWN CLOSE TO THE SCOTTISH LINE.

AN OPPORTUNITY FOR THE HOME SIDE: AN ENGLISH PLAYER AWAY WITH THE BALL, WITH A SCOTTISH HAND ON HIS SHOULDER.

SCORING ENGLAND'S FIRST TRY: A. T. VOYCE (EXTREME RIGHT) JUST ABOUT TO PLACE THE BALL OVER THE SCOTTISH LINE.

"GRAPPLING WITH THE FIERCE OLD FRIENDS": A LOOSE SCRUM AN ENGLISH PLAYER SECURES THE BALL.

TAKING HIM LOW: H. L. V. DAY (AN ENGLISH THREE-QUARTER) TACKLED BY A SCOT AFTER RECEIVING A PASS FROM ANOTHER ENGLISH PLAYER.

The *ILN* was now committed to a policy of two-camera coverage for Rugby football which generally paid off. Pictures taken by a photographer positioned a little way up-terrace, perhaps close to a corner flag, could give superb panoramic moments like the incident in which W. W. Wakefield is felled in the act of crossing Scotland's line in 1926. Notice, however, that the vantage point selected here is at the Scottish end of the field, indicating confidence that this was the place from which to capture vital scores – not on England's line!

The touch-line cameraman chose the same end of the stadium, to be rewarded with a study of Tom Voyce tearing the ball from a Scot's grasp to score a try in his last International match.

Another long-serving Englishman was John Tucker of Bristol, who won twenty-seven caps as a hooker between 1922 and 1931 and is seen here scoring one of his two International tries. England's delighted players raise their arms (below), with the exception of Wavell Wakefield, on left, and Carlton Catcheside.

However, both photographers would have done well to be at England's end, where two Ian Smith tries, a Dykes dropped goal and some accurate place-kicking by Herbert Waddell helped Scotland hold onto the Calcutta Cup. A small piece of history was also made, this being the first time for England to lose at Twickenham to a European nation.

Wing H. L. V. Day won four England caps and reported Rugby for several newspapers after his retirement.

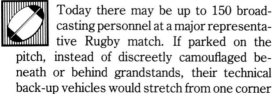 Today there may be up to 150 broadcasting personnel at a major representative Rugby match. If parked on the pitch, instead of discreetly camouflaged beneath or behind grandstands, their technical back-up vehicles would stretch from one corner flag across to the other.

A great oak, in other words, has sprung from the acorn that germinated at Twickenham in January 1927 when England met Wales. Pictured above is the temporary BBC hut to accommodate a commentator, an assistant and the microphones from which there was "broadcast an account of the match during play". Parked below, says the *ILN*, is "a motor-van containing amplifiers".

The experiment was evidently successful. In time for the 1928 Championship season a permanent platform was erected at the southern end of the West Stand where H.B.T. Wakelam held forth as the BBC's first official commentator. In front of him in the box dangled the terse admonition "No swearing".

For that momentous experiment a year earlier the broadcasters picked a game that must have been thrilling to describe. The try scored by L.J. Corbett (top), followed a tremendous break through the Welsh defence which finished beneath the cross-bar and made the vital conversion a formality.

Though they turned on one or two fireworks, such as the acrobatic reverse pass by Windsor Lewis (Cambridge University and London Welsh), victory eluded the visitors as it had on all their Twickenham appearances since 1910. This time the score was a bare eleven points to nine; and *The Illustrated London News* observes that Wales were unlucky in having to play for two-thirds of the game without prop forward Dai Jones of Newport who went off with a broken collar bone.

The *ILN* did not have a photographer at Colombes on April 2, 1927, and so missed what would have been a great scoop – France's first victory over England after eleven defeats and a draw. However, the magazine did the honourable thing and printed an agency picture of the XV which made history by one try to nil. Its scorer, wing Edmond Vellat, is on the ground, left.

The game marked the end of W.W. Wakefield's career with thirty-one caps to his name. He had been in three Grand Slam sides.

Carl Aarvold of Cambridge University (right), last survivor of the England fifteens of the 1920s, was typical of the newcomers who sought to recapture their country's momentum in 1928. They were so successful that by March 17 just one Twickenham victory was required to bring yet another Grand Slam. Their opponents, however, were Scotland, who had won the previous three encounters between the two nations, and the tam o'shantered supporters who flooded into Euston and King's Cross for the game were in no doubt that the Calcutta Cup would be making a return journey across the Border after the final whistle.

H.C.C. Laird (England's youngest player when capped against Wales at the age of eighteen years and 134 days) and Jerry Hanley had other ideas. After the former had opened the scoring with an unconverted try, Hanley supported a great break by scrum half Arthur Young, who ran right up to Scotland's full back Dan Drysdale and committed him to the tackle before supplying a scoring pass. His nippy team-mate, a back row forward, covered the remaining twenty yards to Scotland's line for the decisive try (far right).

Note the upper deck to the stadium's east stand which raised its capacity to 60,000. Even so "HQ" was bursting at the seams.

 Wales's record in the 1920s had been lamentable, especially against England. Eight games had gone by without a victory, home or away, when the 1931 fixture at Twickenham kicked off – and furthermore the visitors had never toppled England at this ground, opened twenty-one years earlier.

The reports make it clear that the Welsh should have banished the bogy on this occasion. The imagination of the huge crowd was captured by Tom Jones-Davies's superb opening try pictured here, followed by an equally good effort from Jack Morley. A rare "field goal", or goal from a mark, by Wick Powell built the total to eleven; while England seemed to become stuck on eight.

But a quite magnificent place-kick tied the scores in the final seconds of injury time. Don Burland had scored and converted a try, while Brian Black had kicked a penalty. With seconds to go the latter, a brawny Blackheath lock, was given a no-hope shot at goal from forty-five yards after Wales had gone offside and, to the dismay of the 15,000 Welsh supporters who had made the trip, his giant kick just cleared the bar. A hero again ten years later, Black lost his life as a fighter pilot in the Battle of Britain.

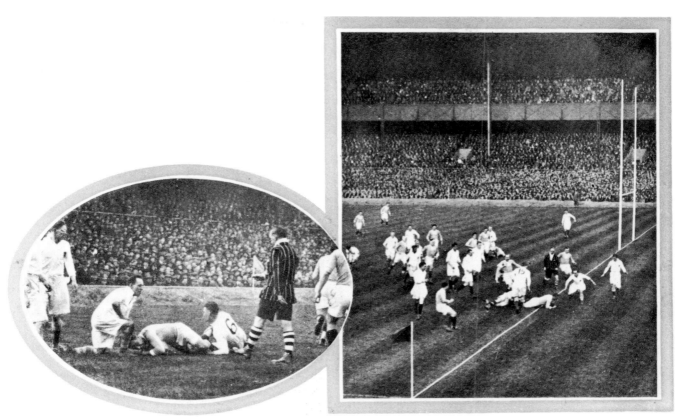

As far as can be ascertained these two pictures represent the first coverage of a try by two *Illustrated London News* cameramen with synchronous pictures from different viewpoints. The scorer is Lucien Serin who, according to the caption, "pierced the defence with a semi-circular swerving run". The little scrum half was one of his country's outstanding players, and from the formation of the players it looks as if he has taken on and out-smarted all England's defenders close to the scrummage.

Albert Ambert converted to give France a sensational interval lead of 5–0. But England rallied in the second half for an 11–5 victory in their last home game against the French until 1947.

In 1931 allegations that France's Rugby was tainted with professionalism led to the suspension of fixtures for sixteen years.

It had to happen eventually. Wales's nine trips to Twickenham up until January 21, 1933, had failed to yield a single victory. On that day a tremendous effort by Watcyn Thomas's team brought a 7–3 success cheered on by 60,000 spectators, of whom, at a fair guess, 15,000 were visiting supporters. Did the feat exact an emotional toll from the victors? This is an interesting point, since Wales subsequently went down to Scotland and Ireland in Swansea and Belfast.

As the dusk of history settles around the game, with only the result standing out like a beacon, it is easy to forget how controversial a game this was. There were allegations that Wales had overdone the rough stuff: Bristol's Tom Brown was kicked on the head and R.A. Gerrard suffered a badly gashed cheek.

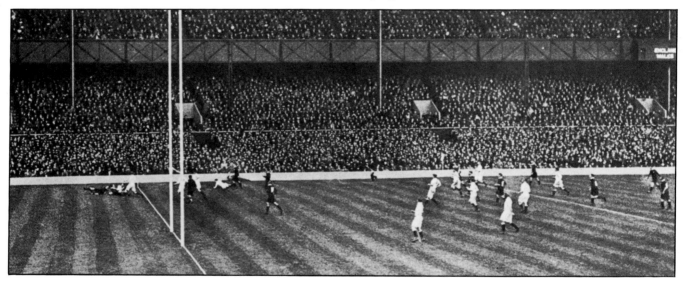

However, the Welsh could claim that Walter Elliott (pictured scoring at the far corner) lost possession of the ball in the act of touching down. After Ronnie Boon scored a try to add to his dropped goal the Welsh touch-judge signalled a successful conversion by Vivian Jenkins only for the English official to keep his flag down; referee Bell, from Ireland, advised the score-board stewards at half-time that the kick had failed.

Jenkins and Wilfred Wooller were at the outset of enormously successful careers for Wales, which were to be cut summarily short by World War II. However, tactical control was exerted throughout by the vastly experienced Harry Bowcott who nearly got through to England's line for a spectacular solo try (opposite).

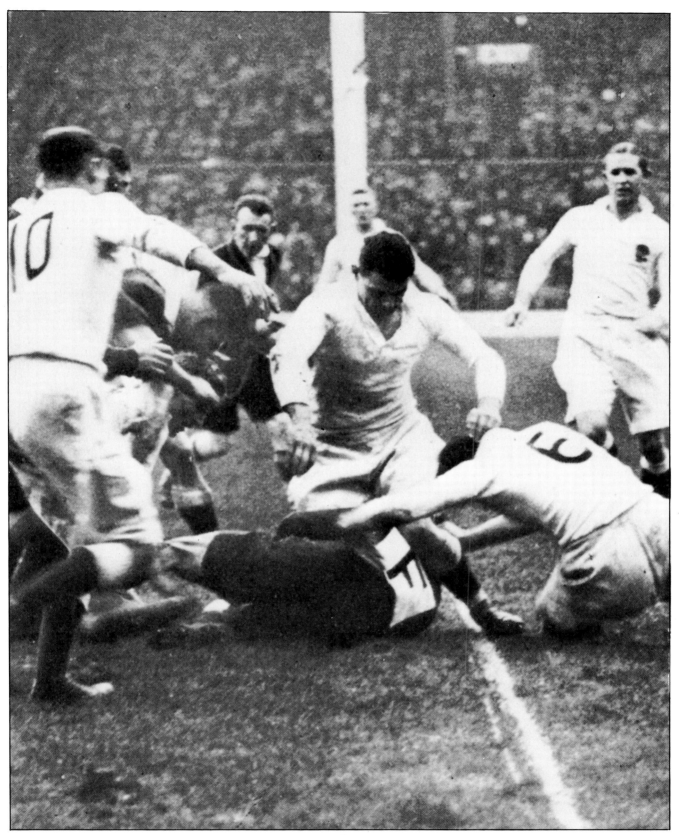

 Ireland had won twice at Twickenham in 1929 and 1931 and, after their team's defeat at the hands of Wales, England's supporters must have been fearing the worst on February 11, 1933. However, a tremendous display by new captain A.L. Novis inspired his team to a 17–6 victory which included five tries.

The skipper himself claimed two of them, and is seen in these studies by an alert touch-line photographer initiating and then rounding off the first score (top pictures).

Novis has evidently been given early ball, and as he crosses the 25-line he is ideally placed to use his celebrated outside swerve to beat the ponderous challenge coming in from his right.

It might pedantically be observed that as a left wing he has the ball under the "wrong" arm. A few yards from the corner-flag, however, he decides to step inside Ireland's Edward Light-foot (number eleven, on ground), at which point he has the correct arm free for a hand-off. Finally, his velocity is far too great for Robin

Pratt's off-balance tackle and the Englishman literally flies in for his try. One of his boots caught the defender's head, laying him out for a couple of minutes.

Pratt is again out of luck (Waide is the other tackler) as scrum half Bernard Gadney gets through Ireland's defence for another of England's scores following a blind-side break from the 25 (bottom, left). It had been nine years since England had last scored five tries, in their Twickenham game of 1924 against France.

Another of the scorers was Ted Sadler, making his début on this occasion and written up as man of the match for "a game worthy of Tom Voyce at wing forward". He is seen here (above), left foreground, with arms poised to dig for the ball. No long career in an England jersey awaited him, however, for after one more appearance against Scotland he became one of the comparatively few top-rank English Rugby Union players to turn professional.

Scotland's visit to Twickenham in 1938 was remarkable for a number of reasons. First, by taking the Calcutta Cup back north of the Border (having succeeded in England for the first time since 1926) the winners rounded off a Triple Crown season, which, had France been in the Championship at this time, would almost certainly have yielded a Grand Slam too. It is ironic that there would be a forty-six year gap before Scotland took the title outright again, with the Triple Crown–Grand Slam triumph of 1984.

Secondly, George VI showed that he had inherited his father's interest in football (both codes) and was in the Royal Box with his wife Queen Elizabeth on March 19.

A third point relates to the media. Hardly more than a decade before the BBC's sound commentary van had made its first appearance at "HQ". Now, in 1938, the King walked out onto the field to be introduced to the teams and, says *The Illustrated London News* caption, was "televised by means of one of the BBC's new super-sensitive cameras which was used to follow the actual play".

What sort of a match was shown to viewers living within range of Alexandra Palace? For a start the *ILN* pictures highlight a problem that television must cope with to this day at the bigger stadia: the deep shadow which, on sunny days, runs directly down the middle of the pitch (inevitable, since early grandstands were sited to save spectators the inconvenience of the afternoon sun shining into their eyes).

However, there was a lot of sparkling action, notably from a wing making his début, Will Renwick. He scored two of the five unconverted tries totalled by Scotland, the highest number they have scored in a Championship match in England. The picture shows the first one, in which Renwick – sadly to die in action during World War II – is being well supported.

The other score is by R.C.S. Dick, the scattered deployment of the players clearly indicating that the try was a spectacular one whose origins lay a long way back down the field – and which would have merited endless action-replays half a century later.

G.W. Parker kept England in the hunt for a while with three penalty goals (to add to the six conversions and penalty goal he had kicked against Ireland: how strange that this west countryman never again played an International match), but Scotland were in devastating form.

The hearts of onlookers (except Welsh ones) bled for Bath's Chris Martin in 1985 when a steepling kick by Jonathan Davies eluded his grasp and let the stand off in for a vital try. A similar fate befell another England full back, Robert Barr of Leicester, in 1932 when South Africa were England's opponents.

After Benny Osler had fly-hacked the ball just above his outstretched fingertips, there was still enough time for Barr to turn and chase back ahead of the attacking Springboks. The next bounce, however, took the ball in a different direction and over the England goal line. Now the South Africans were catching up and poor Barr decided to risk all by hurling himself down to secure a minor. A final unpredictable caper took the ball away from him yet again and beneath the nose of Ferdie Bergh, who touched down unchallenged for the tourists' opening score.

Barr's bad day was not over. In the second half he took a penalty kick which failed to find touch. At first there seemed no danger as Gerry Brand caught the ball "just inside half-way and one yard from touch". The legendary full back from Western Province, however, was never short of ambition and put in a tremendous drop kick which cleared the England cross-bar with something to spare. The home side fought bravely before going down 7–0.

THE CALCUTTA CUP: R. C. S. DICK TOUCHING DOWN WIDE OUT TO SCORE SCOTLAND'S THIRD TRY; AND (LEFT) THE KING AND QUEEN IN THE ROYAL BOX—THE FIRST OCCASION ON WHICH THE CONSORT OF A REIGNING KING OF ENGLAND HAS BEEN PRESENT AT THE MATCH.

THE OPENING SCORE IN THE ENGLAND v. SCOTLAND INTERNATIONAL RUGBY FOOTBALL MATCH: W. N. RENWICK (SCOTLAND), WHO WAS WELL SUPPORTED, DIVING OVER THE LINE FOR A TRY, AN ADVANTAGE NULLIFIED A MOMENT LATER WITH A PENALTY GOAL KICKED BY PARKER (ENGLAND).

Time was running out for Europe in 1939; Hitler's troops were on the march everywhere; and men had other things on their minds besides Rugby football. But the Championship opened on an optimistic note, especially for England, who beat a highly-fancied Welsh XV at Twickenham by one try to nil.

H.B. Toft, seen here whisking the ball back to scrum half Paul Cooke (top), may have been a little fortunate to resume as England's captain after the defeat by Scotland eight months before. However, it is clear from the accompanying match report that by now he had got a firm grip on the job: "H.B. Toft proved himself more than a mere hooker of brilliance; he was an inspired leader who knew how to get the last ounce out of his men." Later Toft became one of the most distinguished of writers on Rugby football.

For Wales the experience must have been a bitter disappointment, for they had fielded a back division brimming with potential. At half back there were Haydn Tanner and Willie Davies, the cousins who had engineered Swansea's defeat of New Zealand four years earlier, Aberavon's brilliant Syd Williams was on a wing, and the two Oxbridge Blues Vivian Jenkins and skipper Wilfred Wooler were expected to provide the final touch of class.

The latter two, however, had the melancholy experience of just losing a vital race for the ball against Derek Teden, scorer of the game's solitary try. After receiving from Toft, the England wing fly-hacked the ball across the line and got his hand to the ball perilously close to touch-in-goal (bottom, opposite). Wooler (C) hopes that a touch-judge's flag may be up; but Jenkins (A) knows the worst!

For the record, Jack Heaton's attempted conversion hit a post and bounced the wrong way for England.

A few days after the onset of war against Germany the RFU decided that all games already arranged, including International matches, should be cancelled until the opposition in Berlin had been defeated. One anxiety was certainly that Rugby grounds full of spectators watching big games might prove irresistible targets to armadas of marauding German Heinkels and Dorniers. To be sure, there was bomb damage at Leicester, Bradford and Blackheath, while in Cardiff the Welsh Rugby Union's brand new double-decker grandstand was wrecked by a land-mine in 1941.

But the immediate threat of *blitzkrieg* seemed to recede; and during the "phoney war", before the Battle of Britain began in earnest, the game was kept vigorously alive at centres like Richmond where a photographer captured scenes from a match between "The Empire" and "The Army".

For Rugby, World War II meant that some of the century's greatest players were never seen in the absolute prime of their manhood. Men like McKibbin of Ireland, Renwick of Scotland, Guest of England and Wooller of Wales were either dead or six years older by the end of hostilities. Another example is Haydn Tanner, the Gareth Edwards of the first half of the century: he was still twenty-two when the War began, but was well into Rugby's middle-age at its end.

Some precious photographs show him at a peak in 1940. First, although the white forwards have given him poor possession, he is unwilling to chicken out in the face of International wing Ernest Unwin's fierce challenge.

"Spring-heeled" is the description which comes to mind for the second picture. The possession is far better and there is no way the Army back row forwards are going to beat the ball on its journey to the stand off half.

Tanner was to resume in the colours of Wales after World War II, first as a Swansea player, then as a member of the Cardiff club. Another who made a remarkable come-back, though leaving it incredibly late, can be seen at right: the Newport hooker W.H. "Bunner" Travers. Having won eight pre-War caps he challenged again in 1949, adding four more to his tally.

Normally players are presented with just one cap, their first; but "Bunner" is unique in owning two. He declares that the official who gave it to him could not believe that he was the same Travers who had last been capped in 1939!

At least Tanner and Travers survived the fighting. Some of the brightest stars in Rugby's pre-War firmament had been extinguished by the cessation of hostilities in 1945. One of them was Prince Alexander Obolensky, the only Russian ever to play for England, seen arriving here with his team-mates for an unofficial International against Wales at Cardiff in March, 1940. The group are, left to right: R.E. Prescott, T.F. Huskisson, Obolensky and E.J. Unwin. (Tommy Kemp, the new captain of England's wartime XV, appears in civvies as a doctor at St Mary's Hospital, inset.)

"Obo", of course, had burst onto the Rugby scene like a comet in 1936 when his two tries contributed to England's historic victory over New Zealand. For one of them he pierced the heart of the All Black defence with a dazzling run that began out near touch at half-way and finished close to the posts.

Below he wrong-foots the Welsh defence at the start of another amazing run. To quote the caption writer: "This manoeuvre began England's last try. 'Obo', making ground all the way, went clean over to the right before passing to Teden, who ran with tremendous power close to touch. His inward pass was followed by a scramble, after which Kemp . . . dived on the ball for his second try."

But, alas, the days of Obolensky were indeed numbered. Just over a fortnight after the capacity crowd at Cardiff Arms Park had risen to acclaim his running, he was another casualty of the War, killed in a flight training accident.

 Ronnie Knapp, the Welsh left wing, kicks ahead in the unofficial International against England at Cardiff in 1940. He appears to be inside the visitors' 25 (as it then was) and his little chip nearly brought a score for Wales – "had he not just failed to collect it again he must have scored the first try of the game, which would have given Wales great heart", says the reporter. As it was, after falling behind, England finished strongly to win by eighteen points to nine.

Knapp was an up-and-coming wing from Cardiff of whom more must have been heard had the War not intervened. Instead, since no caps were awarded for encounters between 1939 and 1946, his is a name which does not figure in the lists of International players – and there must have been many like him, of all nationalities, who would surely have picked up a dozen or so caps in the space of six years. More fortunate was Les Manfield, the nearest support player inside Knapp. This number eight forward gained two caps before the War, won the DFC during RAF service, and came back to play five more times for Wales in 1947 and 1948.

Less than a year after this photograph was taken the North Stand at the famous stadium was hit by a German land-mine which wrecked a large section of it and made many tiers unsafe for the best part of a decade.

Here and there in Britain the game lingered on, with a spectacular inter-Services tournament in which overseas stars from South Africa and New Zealand often took part. The schools and universities, too, kept the flag flying. But for the most part the stadia, like the pages of *The Illustrated London News*, were devoid of Rugby action. There was a more important contest to be won, and illustrated.

# 3
## Golden years

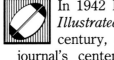In 1942 Bruce Ingram, who had edited *The Illustrated London News* since the turn of the century, produced an issue to celebrate his journal's centenary though, sadly, wartime constraints meant that it could not be the block-buster for which he had hoped. Even after the cease-fire newsprint remained in short supply for some years. Thus newspapers were limited to a single folded broadsheet, and an average *ILN* edition might number a couple of dozen pages.

Sport, however, was quick to demand attention, and with the public appetite craving satisfaction after six negative years many ruling bodies were quick to get their act together. Scarcely had VE-Day been celebrated than Miller, Hassett and other Commonwealth stars were bringing life and vigour back to Lords. England hosted a tour by India's cricketers in 1946 and that winter the MCC sent a touring team to Australia. Yvon Petra swooped to take the Wimbledon title in a jam-packed centre court. Association football, graced by great players like Matthews, Lawton, Cullis and Swift, got its league and International programme back under way, Derby County and Charlton Athletic proving post-War pace-makers among the clubs.

Rugby football appears to have been dilatory by comparison. A series of "Victory" Internationals was played in the winter of 1946, for which no caps were awarded. Full honours were denied to players selected for the Home Countries against the Kiwis, the brilliant New Zealand Services team. Not until January 1947 did an official International Championship programme get under way again.

Curiously, the *ILN* was equally slow off the mark, failing to accord the game the enthusiastic coverage that had been the case in the 1930s and even in the early War years. Only token team photographs marked the return of big Rugby to the great European arenas, and even the presence of the first major overseas touring side, the Wallabies, was acknowledged only by a group shot on the gangplank of the liner in which they had come from Australia.

But swelling crowds and grounds bulging at the seams finally retrieved the *ILN*'s interest. By 1950 the time was ripe, with Wales, in particular, producing quality Rugby and another Springbok touring side due. Also, a new force, France would soon emerge among what had again become the "Five Nations".

 In contrast to their doldrums after World War I, the 1940s saw Ireland dominating Championship Rugby, now a five Nations tournament again following France's re-admission. Dublin and Belfast, the twin Irish venues of that time, celebrated titles in 1948 and 1949 with a Grand Slam and two Triple Crowns.

As for Wales, holders of the Wooden Spoon when the 1950 campaign opened, things could only get better. And yet, despite dismal defeats and unexpected reverses, the atmosphere up and down the Valleys in those days was never pessimistic. It was as if people were just waiting for the brilliant crop of post-War players to catch fire and produce the special something that was felt to be latent.

Twickenham, where Wales had won but once in forty years, was not an auspicious venue for the hoped-for renaissance. Yet, before a record crowd for the ground of 75,532, a new Welsh captain, austere John Gwilliam, proved the alchemist who initiated a mini "golden era".

Among the gilt-edged supporting cast were Olympic sprinter Ken Jones, W.B. "Billy the Kick" Cleaver, Rex Willis and Roy John. But, above all, the day's hero was a bandy-legged eighteen-year-old from Gorseinon called Lewis Jones who rewarded the selectors' daring with a magnificent display at full back.

After England had led through J.V. Smith's try, converted by Murray Hofmeyr, a long, loping run by Jones created a try for Cardiff prop Cliff Davies. The teenager then kicked a penalty, before converting this splendidly photographed try by iron-hard Pontypool forward Ray Cale. *The Illustrated London News* rightly called it "the try that clinched Wales's victory" but England's coach, had there been such a man in those days, would have been beside himself with fury at the evidence of four defenders behind the goal-line and therefore effectively out of action.

In retrospect England tempted fate by choosing a team which contained nine new caps.

 Summer 1950 brought the first overseas tour by the British Isles since the 1938 visit to South Africa. Oddly, considering the full scale coverage it accorded MCC tours at the time, the *ILN* took little notice of this major expedition, which removed thirty amateurs to the opposite end of the world for eight whole months.

Notice had been taken, however, of a device which it was felt could sustain forwards' fitness and improve their techniques on the long sea voyage to Australasia. So here we have a portrayal of some luckless Esher club members panting and sweating at a new-fangled scrummaging machine like mediaeval felons in the stocks, being exhorted by the carefree scrum half on the right. The caption writer quotes the RFU as being interested in the machine "which will enable forwards to keep in practice throughout the long sea voyage". No doubt forwards like Karl Mullen, Tom Clifford and Cliff Davies were thrilled at the prospect.

The idea was not a new one. The Esher RFC

secretary of the day had introduced a scrummaging machine to his club several seasons earlier, but whereas that had been cemented into the ground the model shown here was portable. It weighed under two hundredweights, cost £30 and could be used "on the sports field, in a gymnasium or on a ship's deck".

We do not learn from the *ILN* whether it was wanted on voyage. However, though the Lions lost their Test series, no self-respecting club is without its scrummaging machine these days.

Vital action in big Rugby matches is so compelling that no spectator would dream of glancing away to watch a figure on the periphery. However, the modern generation of Rugby cameramen, like Colin Elsey, Peter Bush, Clive Lewis and John Harris, move up and down the touchlines almost as fast as an average prop forward in their keenness to be in the right place at the right time.

I have a feeling that this fast, anticipatory tradition was founded during the England–South Africa Test at Twickenham in January, 1952. *The Illustrated London News* published six well shot and carefully selected photographs which give the reader the feel of an alert cameraman engaging top gear in order to speed beside the players to capture drama at close range.

However, the first try is pictured by a colleague positioned further away on a terrace. It is scored by tough little P.A. "Fonnie" du Toit, the Springbok scrum half, who got through the England back row from a set scrum midway through the first half. Later (below) the *ILN* photographer snapped a good study of du Toit, short, stocky and brisk in the best traditions of southern hemisphere scrum halves. He was then thirty-one years of age and winning a penultimate cap for South Africa, having taken part in the 4–0 demolition of New Zealand in 1949. He won eight caps – and was on the winning side eight times!

 Hannes Brewis, (above) being tackled by England's N.M. Hall, was the stand off half partner of du Toit and also a match-winning dropper of goals (including the one that beat Wales on this tour). At Twickenham, however, the place-kicks which gave South Africa victory were taken by Hennie Muller (second from right) who converted the Springboks' try and kicked a penalty which bounced in off a post (an attempt by England full back W.G. Hook also hit the upright, only to bounce back infield).

Springbok forward supremacy, however, is best epitomised in this study of the lock Ernst Dinkelmann. Upper-body strength is clear for all to see as he rides the tackle and sights support players for distribution. A great study.

Two other pictures are worthy of note in this ambitious page–spread of January, 1952. On the corner flag: a near miss for South Africa as Chris Koch, one of the most powerful forwards in his country's history, loses possession.

In the other picture, England wing Chris Winn, who scored his side's only try in their 8–3 defeat, is gripped by his opposite number, South African wing Paul Johnstone.

After the tour Johnstone attended Oxford University, where he enjoyed some success introducing Springbok techniques and methods which stood the Dark Blues in good stead.

 The 1951 season, falling between two Grand Slam title successes, was a traumatic one for the Welsh who opened with a 23–5 flourish against England but were not to win another game.

Their discomfiture all began with an astonishing dropped goal by a certain Peter Kininmonth, pictured above on a determined break through defenders' vainly clutching hands.

Wales had gone to Murrayfield as hottest favourites ever, while Scotland, who had lost in Paris, fielded three new caps in a team of virtual unknowns. Stoked by skipper Kininmonth's non-stop exhortations, however, they raised a tremendous head of steam and were very much in contention after half an hour. Then came Kininmonth's amazing kick at goal, from the twenty-five-yard line close to touch. It soared over, Welsh spirits dropped irretrievably, and Scotland strode on to victory by nineteen points to nil.

Kininmonth, clad in the scrum cap worn by many tight forwards in those days, had toured New Zealand in 1950 as a British Lion. But he earned his place in history in February, 1951.

In January, 1952, Edinburgh was again the epicentre of a Rugby shock-wave, this time emanating from France's first-ever victory at Murrayfield. The visitors included eight new caps, but Guy Basquet and the Prat brothers, Jean and Maurice (seen tackling Donald Scott, above left) provided the necessary core of experience.

Scots scrum half Adam Fulton is the subject of this excellent touchline study showing the build-up to a sharp change of direction (above). But more typical of the exchanges is the determination of Pau flanker Jean-Roger Bourdeu who, though unbalanced by Robert Gordon's challenge, is clearly going to keep on running (left).

By this defeat Scotland were plunged deeper into the blackest recession of their whole history. They had just lost six games in succession, including their 44–0 defeat by South Africa, and thirteen more matches were to go by before another victory came their way (over Wales in 1955).

Wales embarked upon their second Grand Slam in three years with yet another victory at Twickenham before 73,000 spectators. But England dominated the opening exchanges, and the post-match changing room depression must have been acute at the thought of the carefully-built 6–0 lead that had been thrown away.

A pairing of two new men on the England right had paid a good dividend by half-time. Albert Agar, the Harlequins centre, gave his country the lead, and then came this fine score by the big wing Ted Woodward, a Buckinghamshire butcher who played for Wasps RFC. Gerwyn Williams is not among the largest of full backs to have played for Wales, and his challenge was brushed aside with ease by the six-foot two, fifteen-stone Woodward.

Wales stayed in contention with a try by Ken Jones (below), but were handicapped by the departure of Lewis Jones to the sidelines for treatment to a thigh injury. When he returned he could do little more than limp along on his wing. Even at half speed, however, Jones could set a few problems for the opposition, and ten minutes into the second half he drew a number of defenders and initiated a counter-attack that was nobly rounded off by Ken Jones with a twenty-five-yard sprint. This time the luckless full back is Bill Hook.

There were still thirty pulsating moments to go, but great performances from Roy John at the line-out and Cliff Morgan at stand off half steered the visitors safely home.

It is clear from these pictures that Scotland were often their own worst enemies during those grim years in the early 1950s. Here, for example, a lone forward tries a suicidal break-out from their goal-line (top), which is under extreme pressure from the Sassenachs. The giant figure of J.R.C. Matthews is about to engulf him from behind, while John Kendall-Carpenter's hands are ready to pounce should the ball run loose. Even that great back row forward of Scotland's post-War years Doug Elliott (second from left) has been taken by surprise at the turn of events.

In the other picture the Scottish midfield defence has totally evaporated before a determined bit of running by Brian Boobyer who has Chris Winn in support on his left and a whole posse of forwards chugging through the midfield. It is lucky for the home team that referee Dowling has seen a forward pass and is turning away to blow his whistle.

England finished with a 19–3 victory, their best result in Scotland since 1931. The Scots were left still seeking a winning combination, and several of the XV who appeared in this match were to go down as "one-cap wonders" in their country's Rugby archives.

The New Zealand tourists of 1953–54 were not in quite the same class as their predecessors of 1924 or as the teams of 1963 and 1967. Early in their tour they went down to a very strong Cardiff XV and lost to Wales a month later. Contemporary critics felt that the team did not play to its strengths, which included speedy wings like Ron Jarden and a great running full back in Bob Scott. However, the All Blacks' chief aim was to recover some of the pride which had been shattered by their 4–0 humiliation at the hands of South Africa in the 1949 Test series, and their selection of a kicking first five eighth, Laurie Haig, for the games which mattered indicated their intention of playing percentage Rugby. When they beat Ireland comfortably in January, 1954, it seemed that they might be on the way back up.

But the capacity crowd of 72,000 which came three weeks later to a Twickenham elaborately protected against freezing weather thought the home team were in with a chance, and it was a bitter disappointment that the England pack on the day could not subdue its opponents' forwards, who won enough possession to ensure that the game could be closed up. Late in the first half a forward rush featuring Kevin Skinner and "Tiny" White ended with George Dalzell crashing over for the only try of this match. Scott placed the conversion from wide out.

The New Zealanders went on to Edinburgh, where they duly beat Scotland 3–0, but in Paris they were the victims of France's greatest triumph to date and lost by the same margin.

 The date is March 26, 1955, the scene Colombes, and France are confidently expected to complete a Grand Slam for the first time by beating the daylights out of a Welsh side whose form through the season has been inconsistent. The French President of the day, M. Coty, is present, expecting to witness a historic feat. But Wales turn the tables, win 16–11, and share the title.

Here visiting skipper Rees Stephens is introducing the French VIP to the twenty-four-year-old Cliff Morgan (at the time working in Ireland and a member of Bective Rangers). Morgan's tactical astuteness led to tries for Alun Thomas and Haydn Morris.

The Rhondda youngster was about to earn immortality in the game as stand off half for the successful and attractive British Isles side that shared the summer's Test series 2–2 in South Africa. For the man on his left, however, his "minder" Rex Willis, it was the end of a career that had brought twenty-one caps at scrum half.

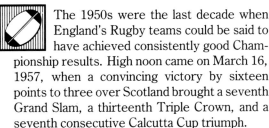 The 1950s were the last decade when England's Rugby teams could be said to have achieved consistently good Championship results. High noon came on March 16, 1957, when a convincing victory by sixteen points to three over Scotland brought a seventh Grand Slam, a thirteenth Triple Crown, and a seventh consecutive Calcutta Cup triumph.

Many England players of that season belong among Rugby's all-time greats. Butterfield and Davies were the centres, with Thompson and Jackson as wings and Jeeps working the scrums. Marques and Currie formed the power-house, with the marauding Peter Robbins here there and everywhere among the back divisions.

But the man chaired off the field at the end of it all was the leader who brought all these rich ingredients to the boil at one and the same time. Lancastrian Eric Evans had experienced a chequered International career in which the selectors brought him in and discarded him at will. By 1956, however, he had beaten off the challenge of rival hookers and, honoured with the captaincy the following season, coerced his men to top position. The following year England retained their title under Evans despite being held to draws by Wales and Scotland.

One of the curses of modern Rugby is untidy possession from the line-out. Aimless tapping and flapping drives scrum halves to distraction (and makes them potential G.B.H. victims of opponents romping through with flying feet). Men like Robert Norster, who can get high enough above his challengers to take a ball two-handed are rare, and even in his case a large proportion of ball is won by one-handed steering, albeit better directed than most.

So it is pleasing to be able to show a past-master of line-out technique in action. In the first picture, left, France are England's opponents in 1957, and David Marques, then still at Cambridge, is a colossus over all the nearby heads. Both his feet are above the knees of John Currie (wearing scrum cap at right; Marques's second-row partner in twenty-two consecutive International matches), who himself stood a full six-foot-three. The throw-in appears to have had a low trajectory, but this fine study of athleticism shows the problems opponents were set.

In the other photograph, from a Trial in 1961, there is a suggestion of "jumping across"; but in those days players could stand a yard or two away from a line-out, gaining height and momentum with a couple of inward steps. Anyway, there seems little chance of Marques being robbed, and again the intention is clearly to get two hands to the ball.

A Harlequin in his later years, the lock finished with twenty-three caps and played in four Tests for the 1959 Lions.

Until the end of the 1950s the Varsity match remained a crowd-puller which could give Twickenham a well-filled appearance. This was partly because until then young Rugby players frequently came up after National Service rather than straight from school, physically more mature and sometimes already the holders of International caps. For instance, by the time his agile reverse pass was caught by the camera in the 1957 battle of the Blues, Andrew Mulligam had been Ireland's first-choice scrum half for two seasons and held six caps. His challenger in the scrum cap, John Currie, had appeared eight times for England while flanker Robin Davies (left foreground) had played three times for Wales.

This annual fixture is always capable of providing an upset, and 1957 was one of the biggest on record. Cambridge's complement of former Blues was considerable and they had marched through the autumn's build-up fixtures triumphantly. But, inspired by their tactically-astute skipper, England back row man Peter Robbins, Oxford kept the play tight to steal a 3–0 victory.

For many seasons Scotland were the envy of the other three Home Unions for the below-ground heating system which ensured that Murrayfield was playable even when the rest of Europe was icebound. Their example was belatedly followed by Wales in 1987.

Scotland's pioneering decision was prompted by the loss they would have incurred in 1959 when their money-spinning match with Wales was threatened by six inches of frost. "Operation Anti-Freeze", pictured here, involved erecting marquees, thawing the turf with paraffin stoves, covering the area with straw, moving the marquees to another part of the pitch and repeating the process! In the event it was all worth while, for the match took place and Scotland won 6–5. But the SRU knew there had to be an easier way!

 The Mias factor made itself felt in Europe in 1959. France had shared the Championship title with other nations a few years earlier, but lack of discipline, cancelling out traditional flair, had all too often been their undoing as they aimed for outright success. Lucien Mias, from Mazamet, brought his team to heel, and at Stade Colombes on April 4 before 65,000 delirious supporters they beat Wales to become undisputed Champions.

It was a curious season in which no nation was able to win away from home, a pattern which was maintained when the French lost their final match in Dublin a fortnight later. A precious point gained from their draw at Twickenham was thus decisive.

Here Jacques Bouquet flips a pass to Arnaud Marquesuzaa ("M'sieu le Bison"). These two had been with Mias to South Africa on France's victorious tour of 1958; and when the latter announced his retirement from International Rugby they stayed in harness as vital members of a French side which dominated the Championship table until 1962.

 What a difference the day makes. The younger generation, used to its good-looking, healthy turf, find it hard to credit that Cardiff Arms Park in the bad old days could resemble a vast quagmire in December and January – not just occasionally but quite often. Soon after this match between Wales and the Fifth Springboks in 1960 a mounting volume of protests from other nations, plus more than a twinge of Celtic conscience, prompted the WRU to set in motion the project which totally re-furbished the stadium and its pitch.

In conditions wholly foreign to them (though

they may have seen water buffaloes at play in one of their National Parks) the South Africans did magnificently to win by Keith Oxlee's penalty goal to nil, with Doug Hopwood proving the key man whose skilled control kept the ball tight in the second half when the Springboks faced the elements.

That night, incidentally, the adjacent River Taff burst its banks and inundated the Arms Park and surrounding streets to a depth of several feet.

But conditions at Twickenham four weeks later were perfect. The South Africans had followed their narrow win over Wales with a hard-earned 8–3 victory in Dublin, and the capacity crowd on January 7 felt they were vulnerable to an England side containing seasoned men like Dickie Jeeps (right), Derek Morgan (tackling J.P. Engelbrecht) and Don Rutherford (kneeling, left).

Doug Hopwood, however, played another storming game at number eight, scoring a try that secured the tourists a 5–0 success. The Springboks completed their Grand Slam in the Home Countries by beating Scotland 12–5.

An interesting juxtaposition was to be found in *The Sphere* for February 11, 1961. Subject to the permission of local authorities, betting shops were to be legalised from May 1. The kind of establishment shown would take full advantage of the Betting and Gaming Act (1960) to bring British gambling out into the open. Note the telephone number, in pre-numerical days.

Few Rugby followers, however, would have put money on the invitation Barbarians XV relieving the Fifth Springboks of their unbeaten record in the traditional finale to their tour. Watched by 60,000 spectators, however, the Baa-Baas ran out winners by six points to nil thanks to the kind of grim determination shown by men like Tony O'Reilly, shown here tackling Mike Antelme.

 For four seasons Richard Sharp was accorded the kind of homage by English supporters which normally only the Welsh grant to stand off halves. He rewarded them with some majestic displays, beginning with the humiliation of a very experienced Wales back row at Twickenham in 1960. Only the draw with France robbed his country of a Grand Slam that winter.

Well taught at Blundells, Sharp was a very complete player who could put over difficult place-kicks effortlessly. This study of him converting a try against Ireland is not only expertly timed by the cameraman; it also highlights the expectancy of youth, with the kicker eager to glory in his success, and the poise and elegance which Sharp brought to all aspects of his play.

In the other picture (below) Sharp is touching down one of the best tries ever scored for his country. It assisted in the 10–8 defeat of Scotland in 1963, which clinched the title for England after four years' domination by the French. The picture merely catches the climax of a diagonal run which began near the half-way line and during which a host of Scottish defenders bought dummies. In the old days of black and white television Sharp's try was part of the action montage at the start of a weekly sports programme, and was the equivalent in its era of Gareth Edward's try in 1973 for the Barbarians against New Zealand.

At the time of writing Sharp remains the last Englishman to have led his country to victory at Cardiff, also in 1963.

 Not a great match, nor a high-scoring one, between Wales and France at Cardiff in 1962. But the photograph, brilliantly etched in March sunshine pouring down over the Taff, is notable for highlighting four of the period's finest players.

At scrum half for the visitors is Pierre Lacroix, a member of three Championship sides and a tough customer. Not so tough, however, as the legendary Alfred Roques (third from left) – inevitably nick-named "The Rock" by his British opponents – one of the strongest props ever to play International football. Born in 1925 he was not selected by his country until 1958 when he became a fixture until the Murrayfield defeat of 1963 after which he bowed out of representative Rugby at the ripe old age of 38.

Bryn Meredith, with the ball at his toes, is ranked among the best two or three hookers ever to play for Wales, and certainly had no peer away from the set-pieces – as a British Lion in South Africa, for instance, he once hooked the ball at a scrum and backed up so keenly that he took a scoring pass at the opposite corner! This was his penultimate International appearance, and he was captain of the Welsh XV.

Keith Rowlands, immediately to the right of Meredith, was a strapping lock forward who could gain tremendous height at lines-out and could cover the ground as fast as a back row player. A series of leg fractures forced a premature retirement upon him, though not before he had toured South Africa as a Lion.

Later Rowlands became one of Wales's International Board members and served in 1986–87 on the sub-committee which set up and ran the World Cup. Subsequently he became the first full-time secretary of the I.B.

A magnificent try at Twickenham by France's Guy Boniface (above): he has eluded six England defenders including Richard Sharp (10) on his way to the line. But this encounter of 1963 ended in victory for England, for whom John Willcox kicked two decisive penalties.

Meanwhile, below, a great Welsh forward is pictured here in typically belligerent mood. Brian Thomas of Cambridge University is the ball-carrier bowling Scotsmen out of his way as he drives remorselessly to the goal-line for his sole International try in twenty-one appear-ances. N.S. Bruce is the victim at left, while Wales hooker Norman Gale is in support at Thomas's elbow.

After his retirement, the big lock's contact with Rugby football was minimal for some time. In the early 1980s he suddenly re-emerged as the team manager of Neath RFC. Under him the club has been enjoying one of the most successful periods in its history, and credit is accorded to Thomas for his ability to identify outstanding talent and attract it to the Gnoll. Jonathan Davies, Paul Thorburn and Mark Jones are good examples.

 In the days before Five Nations Championship fixtures rotated Triple Crowns were traditionally settled in games between England and Scotland or Ireland and Wales. The latter two nations being marginally more successful than the rest in the post-War decades, some epic struggles took place in Dublin, Belfast, Swansea or, as on this occasion, in Cardiff. The date is March 13, 1965, and elated Welshmen are chairing Clive Rowlands from the fray after the defeat of Ireland by fourteen points to eight. The Triple Crown had come Wales's way for the first time since 1952.

In later years Rowlands, one of Rugby's great enthusiasts, became a Welsh selector and coached International teams. However, his career began controversially and persisted in that vein. Given the captaincy along with his first cap in 1963, he has for long enjoyed unwelcome distinction as the last man to lead a losing side against England at Cardiff for nearly three decades. In the next game he kicked remorselessly from scrum half to bring Wales a win at Murrayfield, where some spectators claim to have counted over 100 line outs. The notoriety acquired on that occasion never quite left him, and perhaps this explains the Barbarians' consistent overlooking of his many qualities.

Inexplicably his own country's selectors dropped him at the start of the 1966 season, which cost him a place on the British Isles' ill-fated tour of New Zealand. Great ball winners like Brian Price, pictured magnificently at full stretch (right), did make that trip, and may sometimes wish that they had stayed at home with Rowlands. The Lions were whipped 4–0.

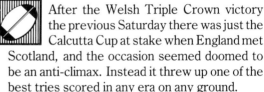

Not quite a try for Irishman Ray McLoughlin, caught on the goal-line by Alun Pask in a match against Wales. The prop from Blackrock had to wait until the evening of his career and a game against France for his sole International try.

However, he is better remembered as the man who revolutionised Ireland's forward play in the 1960s – and actually persuaded his countrymen to train harder and in more organised fashion! The great coach Carwyn James leaned heavily on McLoughlin's technical grasp of front row play during the early stages of the British Isles' historic tour of New Zealand in 1971. It was a grievous loss, from which the tourists did well to recover in the Tests, when he broke a thumb in the notorious carnage at Canterbury.

McLoughlin was already a successful businessman by 1971, and his team-mates christened him "Man at the Top" after a successful television series of the day.

After the Welsh Triple Crown victory the previous Saturday there was just the Calcutta Cup at stake when England met Scotland, and the occasion seemed doomed to be an anti-climax. Instead it threw up one of the best tries scored in any era on any ground.

The game is in injury time as Andy Hancock of Northampton prepares to hand off his opposite number, David Whyte. Scotland are leading by a dropped goal to nil and seem set for a first victory at Twickenham since 1938. Not only are the players camped in England's 25; all the photographers are at that end of the field, too, in anticipation of a second score to sew the game up for the visitors.

However, the powerful Hancock receives a pass from Mike Weston and sets off optimistically, his first few strides caught by *The Illustrated London News* photographer (above). In seconds he has got around a couple of defenders and reached the half-way line in a break-out that

really sets the alarm bells ringing in the Scottish camp. But, failing to recognise the danger, they had begun their frantic corner-flagging too late. Although full back Stewart Wilson overtook him on the Scottish goal-line, Hancock was able to break the tackle and flop wearily over for the three points which tied the game. By that time, however, like most of the defenders, touchline photographers were out of the hunt.

A conversion would have brought the Cup back south of the Border, but it was just off target. What a thrilling finale!

According to the caption to the other picture (right) Alex Hastie is being "forced into touch by [Dennis] Silk near the corner flag". Well, the camera does not lie, and it seems inconceivable that the tackle could have pushed the Scotsman such a distance in the space of a couple of strides. Possibly there had been an earlier infringement, maybe a forward pass, which disqualified the try.

 England received an unpleasant shock at Twickenham in January, 1967. They were looking forward to running up a big total against John Thornett's Wallabies, whose win over Wales was reckoned to have been something of a fluke since Scotland had since beaten them by a comfortable margin. Richard Sharp, England's golden boy of the early 1960s, had been restored to International Rugby charged with orchestrating the tourists' defeat, and all seemed well when England went six points up after ten minutes.

That they finished 23–11 losers can be attributed to a magnificent display by the pair of Australians shown here, stand off Phil Hawthorne and scrum half Ken Catchpole who is receiving his pass. The two New South Welshmen first forged their partnership in the fiery heat of a New Zealand tour in 1962, and by 1967 they had brought their mutual understanding to an uncanny level.

Australia's forwards of that era were none too fussy about the quality of possession sent to the halves, but Catchpole's work at their heels was always accurate. He is remembered for the short, sharp pass delivered in a single sweeping movement which always gave Hawthorne time to choose between options. The latter was a good general, and this photograph indicates how he could draw defenders onto him before releasing the ball.

The 1980s have been Australia's most successful decade, with Nick Farr-Jones and Mark Ella splendid at half back. But the memory of Catchpole and Hawthorne is not eclipsed.

 In photo-recollections of this 1967 match the man on the left is usually depicted sprinting down the North Stand touchline at Cardiff Arms Park to score an amazing début try for Wales against England. Full back Keith Jarrett also put over sixteen points with the boot to total a record-equalling nineteen points.

However, here he can only watch helplessly as John Barton, the tough farmer from Coventry's second row, crunches in for one of his two tries – and in International football that is as rare a feat as a new cap scoring nineteen points. Barton played only four matches for England – but he is remembered at Cardiff!

The game was remarkable in other ways. Played on a bone-hard April pitch it contained a thrilling eight tries and three dropped goals. Wales's score was their highest versus England, and their biggest total since the forty-nine scored against France in 1910. England's total was their biggest-ever in Wales, but was yet nowhere near enough to save them from a 34–21 defeat.

Interestingly, the Australian "dispensation Rule" was to be brought in the following season, forbidding kicking to touch on the full between the twenty-five-yard lines, and was speedily adopted as a permanent measure for the furtherance of open Rugby. But this match, a season earlier, demonstrated a truth: that Rugby football depends heavily on the wish of the players to run and handle – and their mood on the day. Laws can coax and encourage, but they cannot compel locks to score two tries or nineteen-year-olds to run up a stack of points from full back.

The upper deck of a grandstand is the preferred view for most modern Rugby "spectating". That is where you will find the most expensive seats as well as basic positions for the television cameras. It is odd to reflect how dilatory photographers and art editors had been to appreciate the opportunities afforded. *The Times* is an honourable exception: its back page on the Monday morning after a big game was frequently graced by a generous panorama of an important try, photographed from the southern end of Twickenham's West Stand.

So, for *The Illustrated London News*, this is an unusual viewpoint. But what a graphic one, capturing participants' alertness, expectancy, athleticism and aggression. The incident is a line-out at Lansdowne Road, also in April, 1967, where France's win gave them the Championship title outright (thanks to England's defeat the same day in Cardiff).

The picture features some of the game's all-time great performers. Second from the rear, left, is Noel Murphy, a hard back row man who collected forty-one caps for his country. In front of him is Ken Goodall whose career ended prematurely when he turned professional, but who was, for a while, rated the best number eight forward in Europe. Uncompromising Andre Herrero is the Frenchman winning possession against Willie John McBride (face obscured by hands), while the magnificent Benoit Dauga is his impassive team-mate at top right. French forwards in his time were described as "mastodons" by their own Press; and Dauga was certainly one of the herd. His friends and admirers were relieved at the recovery he made from a near-fatal car-crash in 1980.

Though the dawn of the splendid 1970s was not far distant it has to be stated that British Rugby was stale and flat in the preceding decade. With occasional spectacular exceptions matches were dominated by line-kickers like Clive Rowlands and place-kickers such as Bob Hiller, whose two brilliant successes in 1968 helped England retain the Calcutta Cup 8–6 at Murrayfield.

The game itself had developed malignant growths, too, typified by the "pile-up". Players of both sides hurled themselves onto the ground to contest possession in a static, ugly maul from which frequently the ball never emerged. It was lazy-man's Rugby, practised most expertly by the Northern Hemisphere and briefly capable of nonplussing the trend-setters of New Zealand and South Africa. Rightly, however, the International Board's Lawmakers spent much time and trouble in eliminating the pile-up as a feature of Rugby football.

 A French forward gets higher than the Welsh at Cardiff in 1968; the whistle blows for full time and – *voila!* – history is made: France have achieved a major unfulfilled ambition and beaten all four rivals for a Grand Slam in the Five Nations Championship. "Le Clean Sweep", declared *The Illustrated London News* caption, but the French have a phrase for it: *"Le Grand Chelem"*.

Forward power was decisive against a Welsh side that was still immature, but the crucial in-put of points came from behind the scrum. Stand off half Guy Camberabero dropped a goal, kicked a penalty and converted the try by his brother Lilian. The latter's break set up France's other try by Christian Carrere.

 Every now and then down the decades, as we have noted, *The Illustrated London News* has deemed the Varsity match worth a few pictures and maybe an accompanying essay. Often the cynosure of binoculars and lenses has been an overseas luminary like Paul Johnstone or a Welsh wizard like D.O. Brace, just as on this occasion in 1968 it was the gifted New Zealander Chris Laidlaw.

It is an oddity, however, that down the years the judgement of these great men has not matched the maturity of their individual talents. As captain, for example, Johnstone took the field at Twickenham for the game, where arguably the contestants are thirty of the fittest young men in the world, with a cracked and heavily-strapped rib-cage – and lost. Brace, too, was not fully fit when his fancied team of 1956 went down to defeat. And in 1968 Laidlaw took too much upon himself, challenging the

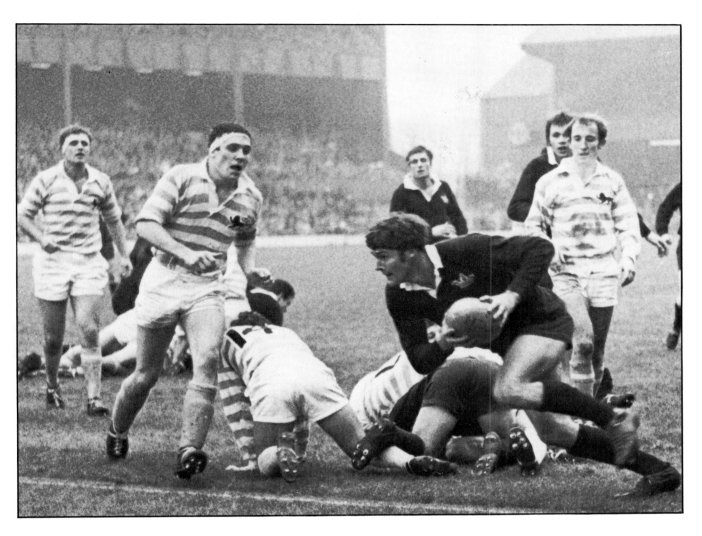

Cambridge flankers, who promptly put him through the mincer, and failing to distribute in the judicious manner demanded by the occasion. With their guiding light snuffed out Oxford became disjointed and frequently vanished up their own back row as in the sad case here of Peter Johnson.

He did score later, however, as did Peter Dixon, poised here to get the Dark Blues off the mark. Viewed from one of the other Home Countries, Dixon's subsequent International career for England was strangely lacking in consistency. It was a Welshman, Carwyn James, who first exploited his talent as a back row forward, taking him to New Zealand in 1971 where he scored an important try in the Fourth Test. But later, though he built his cap total to twenty-two, Dixon was never an automatic selection for England.

Royal visits to Rugby football matches continued to be faithfully portrayed by *The Illustrated London News* as long as the Royals themselves were prepared to turn up. This picture of the Prince of Wales appeared in March, 1969, during a period when the heir to the throne was familiarising himself with the Welsh people and their traditions, the better to uphold his right to use their name. He spent terms at the University of Wales, where he picked up a little of the Principality's ancient language, and his Investiture took place at Caernarfon Castle that July.

And, just as in 1284, when Edward I presented his son to the Welsh, so in 1969 the Celtic tribes still loved a scrap. A few minutes after Tom Kiernan had presented his team to the Prince a fierce battle broke out on the South Stand touchline at Cardiff, just beneath the Royal nose as it happened. A Welsh fist swung; an Irishman was felled, or fell; stern warnings were given by the referee; and people said that had the crowd consisted merely of Commoners there would certainly have been a sending-off.

The Welsh, however, who were on the threshold of their best decade since the start of the century, soon got down to the business of seeing off Ireland by a comfortable 24–11 margin, thereby setting themselves up for a Triple Crown season.

It was a dull week in the late 1960s if a British politician did not snub a French opposite number or the reverse. This was before the United Kingdom's entry into the Common Market, and her Premiers spoke with calculated warmth about the Atlantic Alliance while President De Gaulle riposted with his concept of "a Europe extending from the French coast to the Urals".

Whatever the political temperature, however, it was balmy and springlike when the Tricolours came to Twickenham in February,

1969. A certain desperation could be discerned in the visitors' display, for after winning the previous season's title they had opened 1969 with two defeats. Despite the giant efforts of Dauga, named by *The Illustrated London News* as the star of the pack and here seen crunching his way along the touchline, they were not to break the pattern and went down to an inspired England XV which ran in three tries.

About to challenge Dauga, right foreground, is John Pullin who won forty-two caps between 1966 and 1976 and remains England's most-capped hooker. Though he was a vital member of the 1971 Lions party, Pullin will be remembered by the bulk of his admirers for the two magnificent tours on which he led his country – in South Africa and New Zealand in 1972 and 1973. On each occasion the all-important Tests, in Johannesburg and Auckland, were won. Those victories assisted the Gloucestershire farmer to set a fairly unusual record, that of having played in a winning team against every International Board country.

The pugnacious face of a genuine radical? Or a mischief-maker bent on interfering with other folk's freedom of choice?

The arm of the law, and its protection, were frequently required in the autumn of 1969 when the Sixth Springboks's visit rang down a melancholy curtain on what had been a dull decade for Rugby football (unless you happened to be a New Zealander). Human rights demonstrators against South Africa's apartheid system made the tourists' life a misery and succeeded in focusing the British sportsmen's conscience upon the Republic's problem.

However, often it was at some personal cost to themselves. The incident shown here took place outside St Helen's when Swansea played the South Africans. What had begun as a peaceful demonstration escalated speedily to open warfare between police and marchers, in which ten policemen were hurt (including the local Chief Constable, whose arm was bitten), and sixty-seven arrests were made. Inside, another battle was fought between militants invading the pitch and "vigilantes" posted by the Swansea club. Two-hundred demonstrators later claimed to have been manhandled and injured. The game went on and was won 12–0 by the Springboks.

Likewise, the tour was completed, though five of the twenty-five games brought defeat for the tourists, who set the unenviable record of being the first International Board country unable to win a Test during a full tour of the United Kingdom. Tour captain Dawie de Villiers later conceded that the hostility encountered in many places had affected his team's morale and fitness (demonstrators chanted through the night outside their hotels).

However, the commitment and organisation of the militants served as a warning to major sporting bodies that safety and order could no longer be guaranteed on an inward tour by South African teams, and the Sixth Springboks remain the last to have been to Britain. The violence that flared in 1969 exerted its ultimate sanction in 1987 when the International Board (of which the SARB was still a member) ruled against the proud Springboks's participation in the World Cup.

Not until all South Africans, black and white, have the vote does it seem likely that a reprieve can be earned.

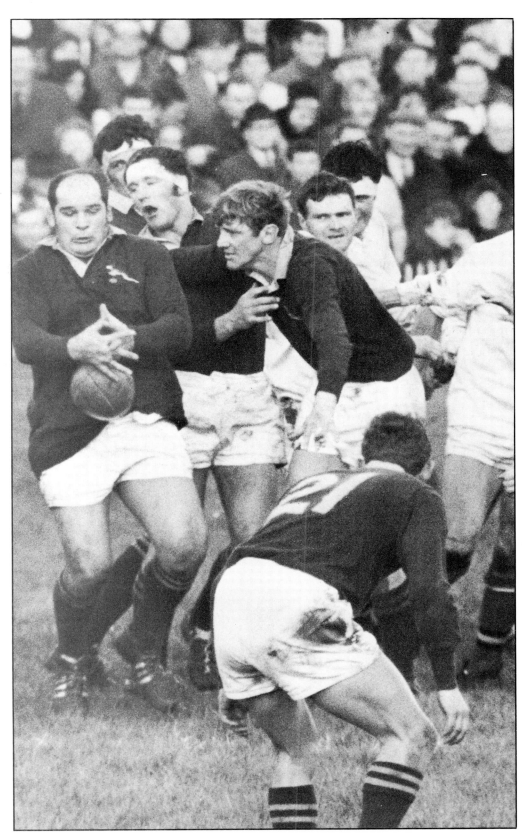

# 4
# The world game

In Europe the Rugby football played and watched during the 1970s was magnificent. Heady success by British Isles touring sides in 1971 and 1974 had put the Home Countries on a "high". The French responded with their traditionally thrilling brand of the game, into which had now been injected discipline and sternness. They and the Welsh enjoyed the best decades in their respective histories, and in teams which collected Grand Slams or Triple Crowns like clockwork there featured a high proportion of the most exciting players of all eras.

New Zealand touring sides, arriving with a regularity which compensated for South Africa's absence, usually wielded the whip hand in crunch games, with one or two falls from grace, while Australia's teams were always attractive if not yet as formidable as they would be in the 'eighties.

Equally exciting, however, was the sudden influx of tours by emerging Rugby nations. Here Wales took the lead (with a National ground now free of Cardiff RFC fixtures and crying out to be used for more representative football), inviting, successively, teams from Fiji, Canada, Japan, Tonga, Argentina and Romania. The newcomers provided tremendous entertainment and, in the case of the two latter nations, robust resistance. Often, too, their tactics were novel and stimulating. During this period people realised that a world cup competition some time in the 1980s would be a possibility.

In amidst all the excitement *The Illustrated London News* was in a dilemma which could be dated to New Zealand's match with England in November, 1967.

This was the first International Rugby match to be televised in colour, and it was immediately clear that from henceforth this would be the major stage on which the game would show off. The colour was brilliant, definition (625 lines) had improved, and the *ILN*'s thunder had been stolen.

There were still some rumbles of resistance, however, and one or two photo-spreads in the very best tradition of the journal. But, perceptively, coverage veered away from the lavish, prodigal use of pictures towards careful selection. Illustrations either had to be something very special, or must relate directly to longer chunks of text. In a way it could be said that it was 1842 all over again: a response to circumstances.

Standards, then, have not been lowered. However, the contents of this concluding section would have been on the thin side without the contribution from outside sources. John Harris works out of Swansea, while Colin Elsey is a partner with successful Colorsport agency. The editor and publishers are grateful to both photographers for the generous permissions to select from their recent touchline coverage.

With the freeze-framing that is a feature of sport on the screen, television directors have acknowledged the fascination of a fine still picture. And down on the touchline it is still possible for a nimble photographer to penetrate the parts that other cameras cannot reach. This truth will never be lost on *The Illustrated London News*, which can also continue to score over its electronic rival through elegant essays for which television has neither the slots nor the patience.

Ushering in a new era of Rugby came the Fijian tourists of 1970 wearing their traditional kilts. The playing record was not an outstanding one, with a number of defeats experienced. Some observers thought that attempts put under way with the best of motives by New Zealand to bring direction and discipline to Fiji's game had not only failed but also proved counter-productive, the natural exuberance having been eliminated.

The South Sea islanders, however, were not the only foreigners in Britain that autumn. Representatives of forty-three nations attended a Grand Congress to celebrate the Centenary of the RFU. Chaired by Dr T.A. Kemp, its purpose was to indicate to the wider world beyond Twickenham how the amateur game was organised in England at school, club, county and representative level. Delegates attended seminars at Cambridge and Twickenham, visited the homes of their opposite numbers, and were finally guests at the celebration match featuring England and Wales against Scotland and Ireland which was drawn 3–3.

Among the nations whose presence was as surprising as it was agreeable were Liberia, Trinidad and Tobago, India, South Korea, Denmark, Sweden, and even Yugoslavia.

January 24, 1970: a historic day for Wales, who escape unbeaten for the first time in seven games against South Africa dating back to 1906. In conditions as foul as they had been a decade earlier, the Springboks, near the end of their last, most controversial, tour of Britain, led by six points to three until injury time when an inspired run through the mud by Gareth Edwards produced a try that tied the score. The scrum half was just off target with his conversion attempt, the last kick of the match.

Reflecting on the game *The Illustrated London News* ignored available pictures of the winning try in favour of this portrayal of the pitched battle fought by the packs all afternoon. Some of the despair and frustration generated by the conditions is etched on the faces of the leading participants. The picture has great validity.

The foreground features two of the finest forwards of recent decades. Clutching the soap-like ball is Denzil Williams, a product of Ebbw Vale, whose steelworks in Gwent, now shrunk beyond recognition, were for long a dependable source of strapping props and locks. Williams, who enjoyed a spell as his country's most capped forward until overtaken by Mervyn Davies, appeared in the second row for his club and operated in the front row for his country.

Challenging him (with the crinkly hair) is another outstanding forward, Johannes Loedwikus Myburgh, known to Rugby folk as "Mof". Having first been capped by South Africa in 1962 he was now near the close of his career, but managed to make two more Test appearances against New Zealand on his return home.

 The 1970s, whose fixture lists were already crammed with colour and novelty as the decade opened, acquired an extra dimension through the grand invitation matches which punctuated it with the successive celebrations of four centenaries. Scotland (1873), Ireland (1879) and Wales (1880) had all followed England's example, and vied with each other a century later to out-do the hundredth birthday parties which took place.

The RFU established the pattern with some magnificent matches, one of the finest of which was that between England and The President's Overseas XV at Twickenham. The greatest players from the rest of the world were im-

ported to join in the festivities and provide some of the entertainment, which they did with relish. Brian Lochore, Frik du Preez, Bryan Williams (who scored three tries) and the big All Black flanker pictured here, Ian Kirkpatrick, were in the team which beat their hosts 28–11.

This study encapsulates both the mobility and the menace of the man from Poverty Bay who went on to captain his country and finish with thirty-six caps (he and Kel Tremain are their country's most-capped flankers). "Kirkie" could flatten opponents like flies or brush them contemptuously out of his path as was shown by his tries against the 1971 Lions (in the Second Test) and against a Welsh XV at Cardiff in 1974.

British Rugby's high noon came in 1974 when the Lions brought an unbeaten record back from their South African tour, having defeated the Springboks 3–0 in the Test series with the fourth match drawn. Here the victors salute welcoming fans, with skipper Willie John McBride at the foot of the steps.

Though this was not quite the end of the road for the Ballymena bank official, who was to play another couple of seasons for Ireland, the picture certainly represents one of Rugby football's greatest rags-to-riches stories. He made the three British Isles tours of the 1960s without playing in or witnessing a single Test victory. The upward curve of fortune began in 1971 with his role in the Lions' narrow but historic victory over the All Blacks, in which the brawny lock earned the respect of Colin Meads. It climaxed with the triumph of 1974 and a final tour for McBride on which he set a record, unlikely ever to be broken, of seventeen Test appearances for the British Isles which, together with his sixty-three games for Ireland, make him the game's most-capped lock forward. He may have been a Lion, but the photograph shows the smile on the face of a tiger among forwards.

Coached by another formidable Irishman, Syd Millar, the team's battering ram was a magnificent pack which for once South Africa could not match. Tactical kicking from Gareth Edwards and Phil Bennett at half back made sure that it was always going forward, and when the ball was spun there were match-winning runners like J.J. Williams, Andy Irvine, J.P.R. Williams and Mike Gibson (just behind McBride) to run in the tries.

The Swansea Valley has produced more than its fair share of scrum halves. Robert Jones, who occupied the position for Wales in the World Cup, is the newest; Clive Rowlands may arguably be the most controversial; but Gareth Edwards is certainly the greatest.

When he retired, abruptly and decisively, after the 1978 Championship season a shock wave ran through the game in the Home Countries and Wales in particular. Among his less disappointed admirers would have been the two youngsters pictured here with him wearing expressions like contrasting masks from Greek theatre, his sons Owen and Rhys. And, possibly, his wife Maureen, long resigned to his winter disappearances to train or play with Cardiff and Wales and his summer absences with the British Lions.

Despite not having featured action pictures of him *The Illustrated London News* marked Edwards's retirement with an essay by Des Wilson summarising his contribution to Rugby and dwelling on many aspects of his career. It began by highlighting his durability – though he was forced from the fray prematurely nursing injury on several occasions he was never unavailable for selection by Wales and his fifty-three caps were won consecutively. He played in ten Tests for the Lions from 1968 to 1974.

The man from Gwaun-cae-Gurwen was also a winner. In his time Wales took the Five Nations title outright six times, and there were three Grand Slams. His presence at scrum half was a key factor in the Lions' defeat of South Africa in 1974 and to a lesser extent in their epic win in New Zealand three years earlier. It is Edwards's only major unfulfilled ambition that he was never on a winning side for his own country against the All Blacks.

He possessed one of the longest services the game has known, which projected partners like Barry John and Phil Bennett, into midfield with time and space to exploit. And finally, despite operating in Rugby's cock-pit, he was an irrepressible scorer of tries, and shares the Welsh record of twenty with Gerald Davies. His most celebrated was the magnificent run-in of the Barbarians's opening try against the All Blacks in 1973, which must hold its own record for being played and re-played on television. But many observers will consider that the greatest was his solo score against Scotland in 1972, which began in the Welsh 25, continued with a chip-kick over the full back's head and ended with a lung-bursting sprint to the corner flag.

 A tremendous study of the power a top-flight player releases into a kick at goal: one of Steve Fenwick's successful penalties for Bridgend against Pontypridd in the 1979 Schweppes Cup Final.

This is a model for any youngster to copy. The left leg forms a platform, the follow-through is full and forceful, and the head has been kept down throughout – thus from the moment of impact the ball is on target for three points. Such a correct method made the Bridgend man consistently accurate from long range.

Fenwick, who signed professional forms for Cardiff's ill-fated Rugby league side at the tail-end of his career, was a deceptively powerful player who became Wales's most-capped centre with thirty appearances. A deceptive loping run frequently enabled him to avoid tackles as he knifed through defences, but if he chose a collision course then woe betide the opponent whose commitment was less than total. He himself was adept at riding tackles.

In the late 1970s an effective Welsh tactic was the sky-climber from Phil Bennett pursued by Fenwick and Ray Gravell – a combination to unnerve many an opposing full back.

 This is a photograph which sums up the tigerish intensity of the Varsity match: the ninety-fifth clash between Dark and Light Blues and the desire to knock the stuffing out of an opponent wearing the other colour burns as intensely as ever it did in 1871. Here Eddie Butler, later to captain Wales from number eight, bears down upon Oxford scrum half Robin Hood who looks to have just enough time in which to get his pass away. Anxiously poised on the right is Dugald Macdonald, who had been capped by South Africa against the 1974 British Lions.

In his accompanying essay Nigel Starmer-Smith, who himself appeared at scrum half for Oxford, observed candidly that fewer Blues than of old were now going on to become International players. Part of the reason he ascribed to "tutors for admission who were not prepared to receive students intent on reading for a Rugby Blue". So the phenomenon of the all-Oxford International three quarter line fielded by Scotland in the 1920s is unlikely to occur again. Nor does the output of distinguished half backs from Cambridge seem capable of ever matching the period between 1948 and 1970 when twelve stand off halves and six scrum halves went on to play for their countries.

Interestingly, Oxford won the fixture more regularly until 1960. Since then Cambridge have been in the ascendant, and in the succeeding years they have won seventeen matches compared with nine by the Dark Blues. However, the number of International players from the two universities, more than 500, is shared equally.

Despite appearing in 1979, the picture is of the 1976 match which Cambridge won 15–0 and was included for reasons of excellence rather than topicality. However, at the time of writing it is the last of its genre – a magical moment photographically frozen at its apogee and allotted the space it deserves. From now on Rugby football's place in the *ILN* is more modest.

 Bill Beaumont and Fran Cotton are on the right. John Scott and Roger Uttley (obscured) have the upper hands at a line-out. And the luckless Scots in the foreground are powerless to prevent England completing the long overdue Grand Slam of 1980, their first for twenty-three years.

Beaumont's triumphant side have perhaps been accorded less than a fair ration of praise. To some extent their season was overshadowed by the Twickenham sending-off of visiting flanker Paul Ringer. This took place during one of the most violent games ever seen between England and Wales; and the fact that, faced with fourteen opponents, the eventual Grand Slam team won by just ten points to nine through a Dusty Hare penalty in injury time raised questions about their true quality.

The side did possess positive virtues, however. Its forwards were a herd of strong, industrious donkeys splendidly controlled and inspired by the captain. Steve Smith and John Horton were ebullient at half back, while the tremendous strike-power of wings John Carleton and Mike Slemen was purposefully released by centres Clive Woodward and Paul Dodge. The aforementioned Hare kicked the goals like clockwork.

So England, holders of the Wooden Spoon as the championship season opened, had triumphantly put a new act together. A foundation of team spirit was laid down on the Japan tour of 1979, after which came the appointments of a new chairman of selectors, Budge Rogers, and a new coach, Mike Davies. At Murrayfield the big reward was reaped.

 The consensus in Wales was that when the time arrived in 1980 to celebrate the WRU's Centenary one particular nation should be asked to ring up the curtain. New Zealand had made a triumphant entry onto the world's sporting stage with the magnificent 1905 tour of Britain; in administering the sole defeat upon the tourists by a try to nil Wales had followed suit; and henceforth there had existed a blood brotherhood between the two countries.

Since 1963 the All Blacks had won seven games in a row against the Welsh, but there was no doubt that their hosts thought the balance might be redressed in 1980, and the proposed five-match itinerary looked as hard as any that could have been devised. The four senior Welsh clubs who had beaten New Zealand down the century were to be met in the space of eleven days, with a Test scheduled for the final Saturday – by which time, thought many supporters in the Valleys, the tourists' heads would be drooping with exhaustion.

Some hope. That is not the All Black style.

From the moment they treated a capacity crowd to their traditional *haka* before their opening match against Cardiff the tourists showed that they were in a special class. After brushing aside the Blue and Blacks they proceeded to take Llanelli, Swansea and Newport in their stride. Though Wales kept them at bay for half an hour in the "Centenary Test", the flood gates were finally prised open and New Zealand's 23–3 victory included four tries. It had been a *tour de force*.

Some of New Zealand's outstanding players of all time figure in this line-out study from the opening game of their 1980 tour against Cardiff. On the extreme left, hands on knees in characteristic pose at the line-out's tail, is the skipper Graham Mourie, who is rated by his own countrymen as one of the two or three best captains in All Black history. He made twenty-one International appearances, captaining New Zealand nineteen times.

In front of him are number eight Murray Mexted, who had first worked in harness with Mourie on the 1979 Grand Slam tour in which New Zealand beat the four Home Countries, and flanker Mark "Cowboy" Shaw, who was out to make a big impression on this his first visit to Europe. The three men formed a well-integrated back row which always worked well with scrum half Dave Loveridge (number nine, foreground).

But perhaps the greatest personality to be seen is the man in possession, Andrew Maxwell Haden, Andy for short. At Cardiff he is the All Black they love to hate – just twelve months before this picture was taken he had been guilty of the notorious line-out "dive" which aimed to hoodwink the referee into awarding New Zealand a last-minute penalty that could win the game (they got it). To the rest of the world he was a "have boots, will travel" figure in his active days, whose passport described his occupation tersely as "Rugby player". It took Haden six years from first pulling on an All Black jersey to win a Test place, but from 1977 to 1986 he was a fixture.

On the losing side can be seen two Cardiffians whose partnership was long and fruitful. Terry Holmes (scrum half) realises that the ball is going away from him, and Gareth Davies to his right begins to move up in defence.

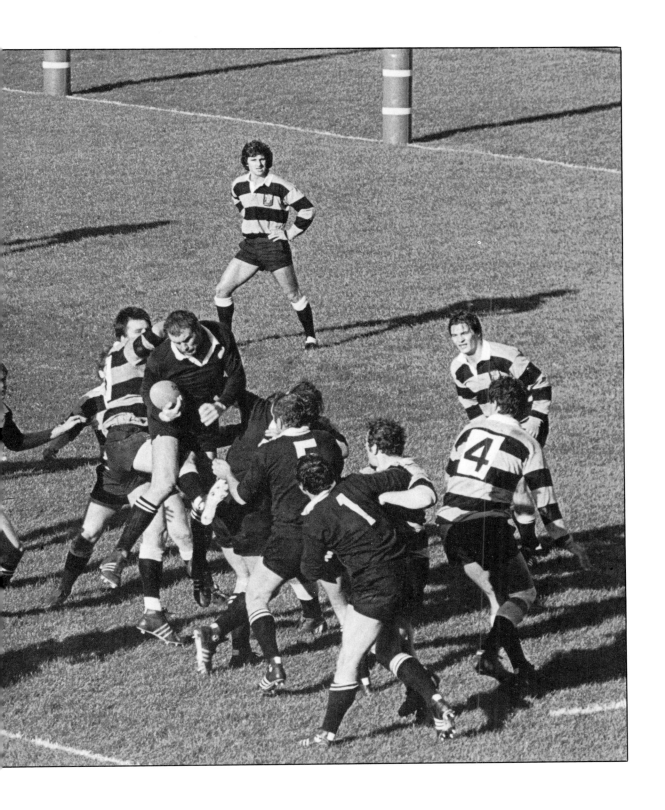

 Queen Elizabeth's visit to Cardiff Arms Park was the first by a reigning monarch since 1935 when George V and Queen Mary attended a youth rally. The 1980 occasion featured a Centenary celebration match between Wales–England and Scotland–Ireland.

Here Her Majesty is being introduced by Steve Fenwick, captain of the "home" team, to Bill Beaumont who had been England's Grand Slam skipper a few months earlier. The burly Lancastrian raised the roof when he scored a short-range second half try.

The Queen was to witness a free-scoring contest in which the Anglo–Welsh combination registered a last-gasp victory. They were trailing in injury time when a remarkable touchline burst from his own half by Terry Holmes led to a winning try and conversion by Gareth Davies for a 37–33 final score-line.

But the most memorable score came from the all-Celtic Scots–Irish blend, after Tony Ward had picked up a loose ball in their 22. He sent the great Scottish full back Andy Irvine streaking out of defence with close support from David Irwin and David Johnston. A swift bout of inter-passing saw the ball back in the possession of Irvine who reached the line for an unforgettable try.

 In its early days *The Illustrated London News*'s Rugby coverage was concentrated on Blackheath, Richmond, Twickenham and centres near the Capital. In the 1920s, as we have seen, giant spreads might feature the opening of Murrayfield or an important fixture against a New Zealand or South African team doing the rounds.

By comparison the space accorded in 1982 to the rebuilt home of Welsh Rugby at Cardiff Arms Park, after a decade of eye-catching Rugby which had filled the WRU's coffers, was

but modest. However, the picture is well chosen and shows the western aspect of the stadium photographed from beside the River Taff. The architecture is graceful, and to idealistic eyes the cantilever supports resemble hands cradling some special inner presence.

The re-furbishing of the stadium is a story in itself. For eighty years it had been used for International matches strictly by permission of occupants, Cardiff RFC. In order to create a national headquarters for Rugby like Twicken-ham and Murrayfield the WRU had first to acquire the premises from the club – and build for Cardiff a new, smaller stadium, whose south stand can be seen at left. There was also a greyhound racing concern, whose dogs com-peted around the Rugby pitch's perimeter, to be bought out. Above all, the playing surface needed radical improvement. This reached fulfilment in 1987 with the provision of under-soil heating to combat frost and stimulate the growth of grass.

From concept to completion the project took close on two decades.

Since the heyday of Richard Sharp no Englishman has established an absolute right to that country's stand off half position. Restless Stuart Barnes, however, here caught on a sharp change of direction in the Barbarians' colours, might have enjoyed a protracted run in the position; but one of the dilemmas this gifted player had to face was choosing between stand off half and full back, since he operated effectively in either role. Sometimes, too, he disagreed about selectorial judgements on him at club and International level and, being a strong-willed character, moved clubs or opted out of national squads.

At the time of writing he wears the number ten jersey for Bath and clearly still revels in calling the shots for that successful club's fluent, imaginative back division.

The other singular twist to Stuart Barnes's career was the sudden acknowledgement of his Englishness. After his birth in Essex the family moved to Bassaleg in Gwent where he was well tutored in the game. He rose up through the Welsh system, captaining the secondary schools XV, and was seen as a star in the making. The disappointment of the Welsh was thus matched only by their surprise when, on the verge of senior representative honours, Barnes declared for England. In a candid moment he said that he had been sitting in front of his television set watching England play Wales when "it suddenly dawned on me that I wanted the ones in white to win". The Greeks had a phrase for it: knowing yourself.

No such nationality "twitch", however, affected this fine stand off half. Huw Davies was born in Eastbourne of parents who came from Maesteg, and considerable Welsh interest was aroused on his arrival at the University of Wales Institute of Science and Technology in 1977, when it was clear that a successor would soon be required in the National XV for Phil Bennett.

Davies explored the available avenues, spending some time with Cardiff RFC, but in due course opted for the land of his birth, which awarded him the first of his caps in 1981. That turned out to be a good year for him: he led Cambridge in the hundredth Varsity match and scored a try in their 13–9 win.

The study is a good one, highlighting impor-

tant aspects of good distribution. Davies has clearly straightened his line, and is leaning into the expected physical challenge from a flanker. The target, somewhere just above the recipient's hips has been sighted, and the ball looks to be one that the centre will run onto.

Until the 1980s Australian inward tours to Britain never enjoyed the same cachet as those by Springboks and All Blacks. The Wallabies had not come with the same regularity; their first visit was in 1908–09 after which there was a gap of forty years (though a tour scheduled for 1940 was abandoned when World War II broke out). Nor did they offer quite the same grim opposition, for the calibre of the Union game was always liable to be diminished by competition from other handling codes: the finest players being turned out from the schools could choose to play Rugby League for big fees or Australian Rules football.

Nevertheless Australia has produced great players – and families of players. The grandfather of Queensland's Paul McLean, pictured here, was a Wallaby in 1905 and 1906. So subsequently were his uncles A.D., R.A. and W.M., not to mention brother Jeffrey and cousin Peter.

Paul, who came to Britain on three major tours, is remembered as a fine place-kicker in the traditional style. Australia's winning score at Murrayfield in 1982 contained twenty-one points from him made up of three conversions and five penalty goals.

If the McLean family is acknowledged to be the most productive in Australian Rugby football, the Ellas are certainly the best-known outside the Antipodes. Glen and Gary won eight caps as midfield players or at full back, and came on the 1981–82 tour of Britain; and this is the beetle-browed Mark, Glen's twin brother and the most gifted of the three.

A Sydney-born Aboriginal, Mark Ella made an early impression on a highly successful trip to Britain back in 1977 by an Australian schools side whose slick back-line displayed all the cardinal virtues. In particular they stood at an acute angle for set-pieces on their own ball with

the result that they ran onto possession at top speed and their wings were in space when the ball reached them. Thirdly Ella was enabled to develop the support running which was a hallmark of his play in senior Rugby. He let the ball go early, and then shadowed his three quarters in order to appear as if by magic at the elbow of a man who needed support. This looping had the effect of straightening the line, as he appears to be doing in the photograph.

Mark Ella helped steer Australia to their greatest triumph of the century in 1984 with a Grand Slam of victories over the Home Countries. In the process he became the first tourist to score a try against each of them.

 By 1982 action pictures of Rugby football in *The Illustrated London News* have become few and far between. Furthermore their purpose is different: far from highlighting a significant moment from a recent fixture this photograph is simply an appetiser to beef up the journal's "briefing" column on forthcoming sports events. The thoughtful articles of yore, with deft selection of accompanying pictures, no longer appear.

If not yet able to compete in its post-match analysis with the best written journalism (outside Wales, where the late Carwyn James had developed a unique approach to the subject) television, with its vivid and colourful action, was by now the dominant purveyor of pictorial Rugby coverage. Also to be taken into account was competition from specialist magazines devoted to Rugby football, which began featuring lavish photo-spreads of a quality which had once been the prerogative of the *ILN*.

But the magazine's staff still had an eye for picture composition and meaningful action, and here selected the moment of confrontation between two magnificent players. The challenge of Fergus Slattery (right) has not been quite enough to prevent Wallaby skipper John Hipwell getting away a touch kick to help his side towards their 1981 victory over Ireland in Dublin. The former is Ireland's most-capped flanker, with sixty-one appearances, while Hipwell overcame a series of severe injuries to top the list of scrum halves who have played for Australia, finishing with thirty-four caps.

 As vigorously as ever they had on their first visit to Britain in 1888, the Maoris of 1982 gave their version of the *haka* before taking on Swansea at St Helens. In the best front row tradition Scott Crichton (sixth from right) finds it hardest to get aloft!

Managed by the magnificent All Black flanker of the 1960s Waka Nathan the Maoris played seven games in Wales without ever asserting their superiority in the manner of full New Zealand sides. Nonetheless the entertainment value they gave was never in question, and big crowds came to see the skills of backs like Steve Pokere, Arthur Stone and Eddie Dunn, all of whom were All Blacks.

Their hosts often wondered why Maori sides as such did not travel to Europe more often. Certainly these colourful characters, with their unique blend of South Sea exuberance and All Black discipline, would like to tour more often away from Western Samoa, Tonga and Fiji and they would be welcome visitors. It may be that the NZRU itself is not anxious for Maori Rugby to acquire the prominence from which a racial rift could develop in the New Zealand game.

Just as in the 1950s David Marques reigned supreme as the top British exponent of line-out play, so Allan Martin was a dominant figure two decades later. In this magnificent study he wears the "Wizard" emblem of his club, Aberavon, for whom he made over 600 appearances in a remarkable twenty-year time-span. Once or twice he veered away in the directon of other teams but he always came back to the club that nurtured him. Today he is a businessman in Port Talbot, one of the United Kingdom's great steel towns.

Technically Martin was a magnificent line-out forward. Where lesser performers might use their stronger, outside arm, only to fall foul of the referee and be penalised for barging an opponent with the loose one, note how the inside arm is being used here making sure that the jump is legitimate and seen to be so. Despite the possibility of airborne collision the player's eyes are open and fixed on the ball.

Martin won thirty-four caps between 1973 and 1981, in which year many people (including the man himself) considered that he had been prematurely discarded by the Welsh selectors. However, he became and remains his country's most capped lock forward and was also a British Lion in 1977 and 1980.

A product of Cardiff Training College (lately known as the South Glamorgan Institute) he was a fine all-round athlete whose six-feet five inches helped him to excel at basketball, a game which he always said all Rugby players should take up to improve their handling. An ability to kick goals from all ranges made him his club's record scorer, a status which he enjoyed for many years, and he also placed penalties and conversions for Wales, notably against England in 1975. In Wales's next game at Murrayfield his touchline attempt to convert a last-gasp try drifted just wide to deny the visitors a draw.

 A picture that sums up the technique and speed of a fine scrum half: the ball and the service just out of reach of the despairing grasp of the back row forward.

David Bishop was British Rugby football's stormy petrel in the 1980s, a man who made headlines off the sports pages in a way that only soccer stars among sportsmen had previously accomplished. Uneasy rumours clung to him like iron filings on a magnet, though they were always dismissed contemptuously at Pontypool behind whose pack he played.

And there was the other, brilliant side to the man, epitomised in this study. He could swing out a service as fast and accurate as any in the world. He attacked fearlessly close to the scrum and frequently left opposing back rows stranded and scratching their heads. He scored an amazing try against the Wallabies on his sole appearance for Wales, jack-knifing and juggling his way over the line at the end of a game in which the Welsh were well beaten. And all this after breaking bones in his neck at the age of twenty and returning to Rugby against the best medical advice.

Opinion was polarised about his attitudes, but about his onfield ability and athleticism there was never argument.

A magnificent evocation of forward confrontation under floodlights as Swansea and the 1984 Wallabies dig their heels in to contest scrummage ball. The steam rising above the sixteen he-men shoving their guts out graphically captures the energy release.

Latterly Swansea, good-looking on paper with regular complements of International players, have found difficulty in rising to big occasions, and although the 1984 Australians were not always impressive outside the Tests they found no difficulty in building a solid lead on this particular evening. Full back Roger Gould put sky-climbing kicks up into the darkness over St Helens, and the All Whites found themselves overrun by the swift follow-up of the beefy opponents shown here with backs to the camera.

Swansea's final whistle blushes, however, were hidden by an electrical failure which extinguished the floodlights with a quarter of the match to go and Australia 17–0 ahead. Players and spectators hung around hopefully for a while until it became clear that, in the short term at least, nobody could produce a length of sufficiently robust fuse wire!

Before the match onlookers were treated to the sight of the controversial Wallaby coach Alan Jones pepping up his team. While his track-suited boys did their bends and stretches behind the dead ball line Mr Jones moved among them exhorting and encouraging. No track suit for this smoothy, however: trim gaberdine and rolled umbrella were the order of the night.

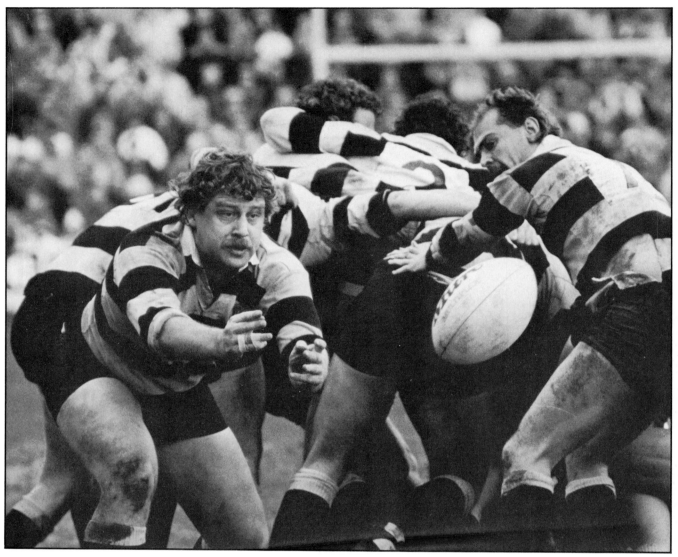

 One of Rugby football's larger-than-life characters of the 1980s in action for Cardiff: exile John Scott flicks the ball up from the back of a scrummage towards his scrum half.

England's most capped number eight forward, Scott caused a stir when he reversed an age-old trend and actually turned his back on London club Rugby, and Rosslyn Park in particular, to temper and hone his play in the hurly-burly of the big Welsh circuit. A few feathers were ruffled at Cardiff when the terse, loose-limbed, Devonian came to the Arms Park, but he settled down to follow in the footsteps of Frank Hancock, Gwyn Nicholls and later immigrants such as Barry Nelmes. In due course, like all these earlier West Countrymen,

Scott finished by captaining the Blue and Blacks. More, he made history by becoming the only man to lead Cardiff for four seasons, in three of which they won the Schweppes Cup.

A master of the number eight game who learned to husband his energies as the years went by, Scott was still available for the club in the 1987–88 season at the age of 33. He also carved a reputation for being free with comment and ready to speak out controversially on issues where his selection committee would have preferred discretion.

The photograph captures the bulk and weight of Scott, braced against possible challenge and shielding the ball. Another International player of recent seasons, Gareth Roberts, turns before leaving to back up the attack.

 John Scott again, now in the white strip of England – but this time it looks as if he will have to give best to his Irish rival. However, the photograph manages to pose the eternal line-out conundrum: whose hand is higher and stronger? On which side will the ball descend?

*The Illustrated London News* has paid few visits to Lansdowne Road, but a salute to the achievement of March, 1985, was in order. For the second time in three years the Irish, led by hooker Ciaran Fitzgerald, swept to a Triple Crown with a 13–10 victory over England. The hard graft, however, was really done away from home with an unlikely brace of triumphs in Cardiff and Edinburgh. A draw against France in Dublin prevented a Grand Slam, which would have been only the second in Irish history.

With that, action coverage of Rugby football more or less pauses for breath in the *ILN*, with new journalists and picture editors in charge – and perhaps an evolving readership – waiting to see which way the wind will blow, where taste will take them, how coverage of big sport will develop and what gaps TV will leave unfilled.

Thanks to the remarkable tournament staged in the summer of 1987 this book about Rugby football's ever-evolving scene can finish on a triumphant note. The World Cup, with its four attractive preliminary Pools and venues shared between New Zealand and Australia, was a huge gamble by the administrators of what has been arguably the world's most conservative sport. It was also a gamble that paid off with a month of dynamic and compelling play gracing not only the big arenas of New Zealand and Australia but also the television screens of the world. Top photographer Colin Elsey was at many of the finest games, including the crowd-pulling opener in Pool One between England and Australia.

This picture encapsulates much that was special about the whole competition, in which flair and determination were two key factors. England's new captain, Mike Harrison, has been knocked sufficiently off course by Brett Papworth's last-ditch tackle to prevent him adding a second try to the one converted by Jonathan Webb which kept the underdogs in with a chance at 6–6 until ten minutes into the second half. A tremendous frozen moment in time, just missed by the amateur photographer at right.

England's victory hopes were wrecked by a David Campese try awarded by New Zealand referee Lawrence but deemed invalid by almost everyone else who had a view of it. The Wallabies went on to a 19–6 win that flattered them.

Harrison lifted his men for the two remaining Pool matches, in which ten tries were run in against Japan and four against the USA. But their exit from the competition followed at the quarter-final stage with defeat by sixteen points to three at Welsh hands. That day England were unrecognisable as the country which had run Australia so close.

Australia had been rated joint favourites with New Zealand at the outset of the World Cup. The expectation was that, having brushed France aside in the semi-final at the Concord Oval in Sydney on June 13, the Wallabies would proceed to the Final in Auckland and a showdown with the All Blacks.

France, having put a colossal effort into winning their Five Nations Grand Slam, said modestly that they expected to reach the semi-final stage, but that it would be a bonus to go further. In the event they rose to the occasion, and in a quite outstanding game out-scored the Australians by four tries to two, running up twenty-four points in the second half for a 30–24 victory.

Here is the end of Serge Blanco's tre-mendous injury-time sprint which clinched the result. The full back from Biarritz had to show pace and determination to outstrip desperate defenders, of whom hooker Tom Lawton came closest to saving the day. Blanco had frequently put French supporters' hearts in their mouths with his laid-back approach to the workaday chores of defence, but as so often in big games he pulled out something special when it was really needed.

Rugby men are supposed to say sportingly that they would rather lose a high-scoring, entertaining game than win a bad one. However, Australian skipper Andy Slack was more candid in his reaction to the match: "I would rather we had won 3–0 and had most of the crowd snoring than lose like that," he declared.

 In a sense France had played their "Final" against Australia and could summon up no fresh resources to meet the might of New Zealand in a one-sided match at Auckland where they went down by twenty-nine points to nine.

Thus ultimately the first World Cup is remembered for the awesome power and technical expertise of the All Blacks, which was by no means confined to the scrummage. Aucklander John Kirwan proved himself as fine a wing as ever wore the silver fern, using smart footwork or block-busting tactics as he felt inclined. Here he crosses for one of his two tries in New Zealand's 49–6 rout of Wales. Kirwan also scored in the Final, while his try against Italy in a Pool match (one of a dozen by the All Blacks) was an amazing effort from long range even allowing for some ill-directed tackling.

At six-feet four inches Kirwan is the tallest wing ever to represent New Zealand. Still only twenty-two during the World Cup, he seems destined to go down as one of Rugby football's all-time great backs.

In the final analysis, however, the World Cup was dominated by forward play on New Zealand's part as shattering to opponents as any seen down the century. Their rucking was at its slick, mechanical best, while McDowell, Fitzpatrick and Drake gave the front row of the scrummage a solidity some All Black packs had lacked in the past.

The present generation of New Zealander forwards, however, seems cast in a different mould from the rest of the world. Other nations fielded second row forwards who were either powerful but ponderous or rangy and vulnerable. Gary Whetton (top, right) typified the lock forward custom-built for the 1980s with an insatiable appetite for running and handling at speed, and an armour-plated physique which made him formidable in tighter exchanges.

The other fine studies feature Andy Earl in full cry for one of New Zealand's six tries against Argentina (far right), vainly pursued by the Pumas' ageing play-maker Hugo Porta. Mark Brooke-Cowden (near right) has the Welsh line in his sights, and no one, including Dick Moriarty (left), is going to prevent him crossing it.

And, fairly snorting hostility and venom, number eight forward Wayne Shelford, judged by many people to have been New Zealand's player of the tournament. The man from North Harbour proved himself a worthy successor to Murray Mexted.

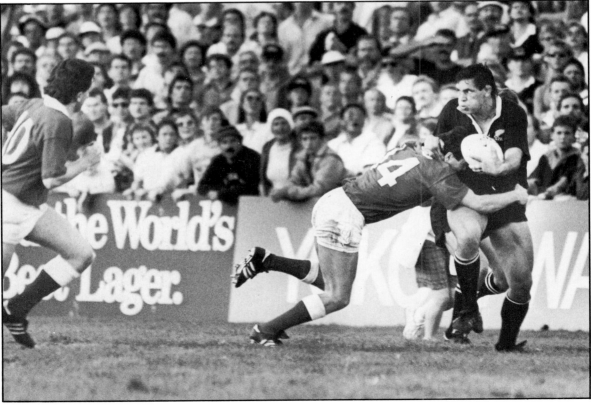

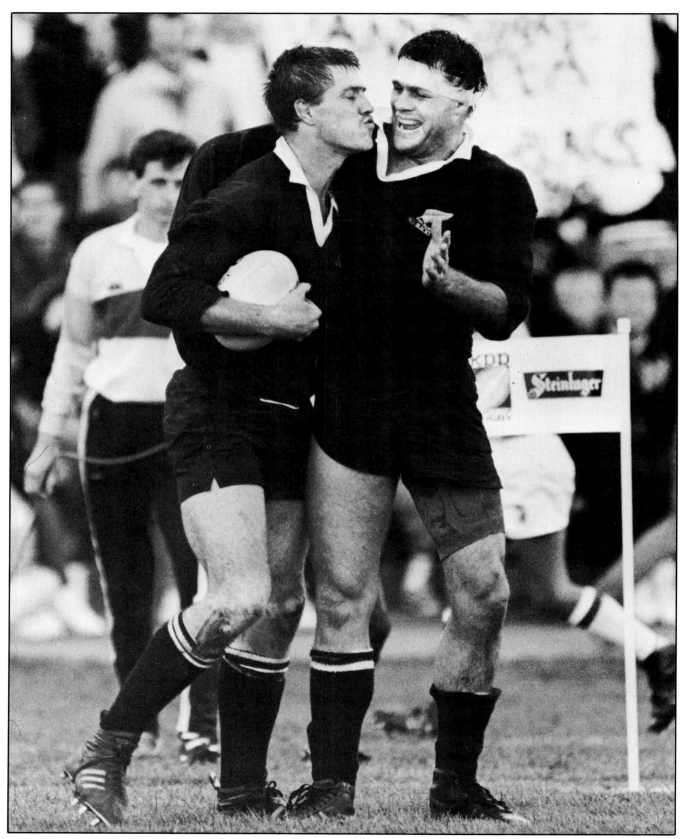

And at the end of a game when you've proved yourself men among men and one of you has just received a scoring pass from the other, what's the harm in a quick show of real appreciation!

Andy Earl and Richard Loe are the All Blacks heaping congratulations upon each other.

In the end it was the All Blacks, led by scrum half David Kirk, who became the first holders of the William Webb Ellis trophy. Their victory over France in the World Cup Final by twenty-nine points to nine was hard-earned but decisive and typical of the heavy scoring they had registered throughout the competition. But despite the yawning gap between New Zealand and the rest there was general acclaim for a tournament that had been thoughtfully organised and highly successful. Scarcely had the final whistle blown than people started talking about staging the next one, in Europe during 1991, a proposal which quickly received official approval.

The competition also represented a milestone along the slow process of popularisation which had been proceeding for more than a century. The game was now exposed to bracing winds of change blowing from North and South America, central and northern Africa, the Far East and from behind the Iron Curtain.

What a contrast with the cautious gradualism that had gone before. Originally just four nations had shaped Rugby football's destiny. For many decades the International Board, or ruling body, comprised no more than seven powers, even France being made to serve a long, long apprenticeship before being allowed to share control of the game.

From the evidence of this volume, however, it is clear that *The Illustrated London News* can claim to have played a major role in drawing the game to the attention of an ever-broadening audience. Its artists plodded the touchlines at remote public schools to depict Rugby football's germination and followed "old boys" to suburban clubs or outposts of empire. Its photographers portrayed early international contests and travelled with great touring sides around the stadia that were springing up to accommodate the crowds wanting to watch matches. Its picture editors developed an unerring instinct for selecting and displaying the moments that mattered. In the middle of the twentieth century the *ILN*'s photo-spreads were a dominant feature of Rugby coverage.

However, it is unlikely that the printed page – even the illustrated page – will ever threaten the position now acquired by television as the premier portrayer and archivist of sporting events. For reasons of policy and an evolving readership the *ILN* cannot be expected to return to the flamboyancy of yore to mount a challenge. Time and tastes have rolled on.

But the journal's part as a witness to the rise and rise of Rugby football can never be denied. In a real sense *The Illustrated London News* is part of the game's essential history.

# PICTURE ACKNOWLEDGMENTS

The author and publishers are grateful to the following sources for their help in providing the additional illustrations (all other pictures are from the Illustrated London News Library).

**All-Sport**   177
**Associated Press**   124, 134
**Associated Sports Photography**   147, 157
**BBC Hulton Picture Library**   18
**Colorsport**   158, 168, 178, 180, 181, 182 (2), 183 (2), 184
**John Harris**   155, 159, 161, 164, 165, 170, 172, 173, 176

**Photosource**   125, 144, 150
**Press Association**   146, 153, 162, 166, 167
**The Scotsman**   140
**Sport and General**   106, 109 (2), 110 (2), 111 (2), 117, 119, 132, 133, 134 (2), 136, 137, 141, 142, 143